Advance Praise for *How Full Is Your Bucket?*

"In this brief but significant book, the authors, a grandfather-grandson team, explore how using positive psychology in everyday interactions can dramatically change our lives."

– Publishers Weekly

"Kindness really *is* contagious."

– Ladies' Home Journal

"A bucketful of miracles . . . Clifton and Rath offer a prescription for reversing the trend toward negativity currently endemic to the American workplace . . . The lessons contained in *How Full Is Your Bucket?* provide tangible, actionable steps to help turn your workplace into a bustling bastion of positivity and productivity."

– Selling Power magazine

"A well-researched, strong, and compelling case for improving self-esteem, better relationships, and health . . . this book is a short, sharp, 'how-to' guide."

– People Management magazine

"Clifton and Rath paint a compelling picture of the good things that happen when people are encouraged, recognized, and praised regularly, as well as the emotional, mental, and sometimes even physical devastation that can occur in the absence of such positive encounters . . . Leaders who want to eliminate or avoid this kind of destruction should make *How Full Is Your Bucket?* required reading for themselves and their people."

– John C. Maxwell's Leadership Wired

"Useful anecdotes that managers in particular should pay attention to."

– The San Francisco Chronicle

"A slim, simple, upbeat volume that manages to be inspirational without preaching (or inducing nausea)."

– The Miami Herald

"The Grandfather of Positive Psychology, Don Clifton, and his grandson, Tom Rath, offer illuminating wisdom for fulfilling work and for a meaningful life."

– Martin E.P. Seligman, Ph.D.
Former President of the American Psychological Association
and author of the best-selling books Authentic Happiness
and Learned Optimism

"Wow! This little book is a treasure. It is chock full of wisdom, inspiration, and practical advice, rooted in solid research. It will change the way you look at your life, your work, and the world."

– Martin Walsh
Executive Director, Society for Human Resource Management
(SHRM) Foundation

"Tom Rath and Don Clifton have nailed it. Their positive strategies are immensely powerful."

– Michael W. Morrison, Ph.D.
Dean, University of Toyota

"The world would be a better place if EVERYONE read it."

– James C. Wright
Former Speaker of the U.S. House of Representatives

"Powerful, captivating, and easy to read. This book's heartwarming message has a spiritual quality, yet it is grounded in decades of research."

– Lea E. Williams, Ed.D.
Executive Director, National African-American
Women's Leadership Institute, Inc.

"I loved reading this book and highly recommend it. I'm buying copies for those I love and care about the most."
— Paul Higham
Former Chief Marketing Officer, Wal-Mart Stores, Inc.

"A powerful experience for every reader and an invaluable tool for energizing every enterprise."
— William Robertson
Chairman, Weston Solutions, Inc.

"If there were a Nobel Prize for building a quality individual, this book deserves it."
— Mike Johanns
Governor, State of Nebraska

"Should be required reading for every company, every school's curriculum, and every couple's premarital counseling."
— Gary F. Russell, Ed.D.
CEO, Major League Soccer Camps

"Filled with powerful illustrations and practical applications, *How Full Is Your Bucket?* is a must for everyone's personal and business library."
— Peter J. Watson
Corporate Learning Coach, Fairmont Hotels & Resorts

"This book reaffirms the value of caring and compassionate relationships. Tom Rath and Don Clifton have created simple, but powerful, strategies for transforming the business of work and finding the beauty in life."
— N. Joyce Payne
Founder, Thurgood Marshall Scholarship Fund

"The book is a quick and memorable read. It should be part of the core curriculum for any corporation trying to build a positive culture."
— Val J. Halamandaris
President, National Association for Home Care

HOW FULL IS YOUR BUCKET?

Positive Strategies for Work and Life

TOM RATH AND DONALD O. CLIFTON, PH.D.

GALLUP PRESS
New York

GALLUP PRESS
1251 Avenue of the Americas
23rd Floor
New York, NY 10020

ISBN 1-59562-001-X

First Printing: 2005
10 9 8 7 6 5 4 3 2 1

This edition of *How Full Is Your Bucket?* cannot be purchased in retail outlets.

To order, call 1-800-425-0726.

*— In memory of my grandfather, coauthor, and mentor,
Don Clifton (1924-2003)*

Table of Contents

Introduction

In the early 1950s, my grandfather, Don Clifton, was teaching psychology at the University of Nebraska when he noticed a major problem: The field of psychology was based almost entirely on the study of *what is wrong* with people.

He began to wonder if it would be more important to study *what is right* with people.

So, over the past five decades, Don and his colleagues conducted millions of interviews, focusing on the positive instead of the negative.

Early in his research, Don discovered that our lives are shaped by our interactions with others. Whether we have a long conversation with a friend or simply place an order at a restaurant, every interaction makes a difference. The results of our encounters are rarely neutral; they are almost always positive or negative. And although we take these interactions for granted, they accumulate and profoundly affect our lives.

During the course of Don's work in the 1990s, a new field of study emerged: Positive Psychology, which focuses on *what is right* with people. Today, many of the world's leading scientists study the effects of positive emotions.

In 2002, Don's pioneering work was recognized by the American Psychological Association, which cited him as the Grandfather of Positive Psychology and the Father of Strengths Psychology. That same year, Don learned that an aggressive and terminal cancer had spread throughout his body. Knowing his time was limited, he spent his final months doing what he did best and what people who knew him well would have expected: helping others focus on the positive.

Although Don had already written several books, including the bestseller *Now, Discover Your Strengths*, he asked me to join him in writing one last book — one based on a theory he created in the 1960s. People had been asking Don to write this book for decades as a result of the theory's popularity. Over the last 40 years, more than 5,000 organizations and 1 million people have applied this theory. And people always passed it along to friends, colleagues, and loved ones.

Based on a simple metaphor of a "dipper" and a "bucket," Don's theory carried profound implications and simplified his life's work for others. So in his final months, Don and I worked night and day to assemble the most compelling discoveries he had gathered over half a century of work. Although Don was undergoing chemotherapy and radiation, we continued to work on this book whenever he had the energy — which was the majority of the time.

We sat in his study for hours, reviewing the research, statistics, and stories we thought you would find compelling. As Don's health deteriorated, I read sections to him and took notes on his feedback. He reviewed every section, wanting each story and insight to resonate with you.

For my part, I was honored to be Don's partner in creating this book. He was my mentor, teacher, role model, and friend. We were exceptionally close, and I cherished the time we had together. I was always motivated and inspired by his vision. And Don knew that I had been touched deeply by this theory throughout my life. As we will describe in Chapter Four, applying Don's Theory of the Dipper and the Bucket energized and possibly saved me in my own battles with cancer.

In hindsight, I think this project also gave Don additional energy in the final stages of his fight with cancer. He had spent his life trying to make the world a better place — one person at a time — and he understood that completing this book would make a difference. We finished our first draft of this book just weeks before his death in September 2003.

Over the 79 years of Don's life, he touched millions of individual lives through his books, teaching, and the global business he built. Don reached so many people as a result of his unwavering belief in helping individuals and organizations focus on *what is right*.

As you read this book, we hope that you will discover the power of bucket filling in your own life.

— Tom Rath

The Theory of the Dipper and the Bucket

Each of us has an invisible bucket. It is constantly emptied or filled, depending on what others say or do to us. When our bucket is full, we feel great. When it's empty, we feel awful.

Each of us also has an invisible dipper. When we use that dipper to fill other people's buckets — by saying or doing things to increase their positive emotions — we also fill our own bucket. But when we use that dipper to dip from others' buckets — by saying or doing things that decrease their positive emotions — we diminish ourselves.

Like the cup that runneth over, a full bucket gives us a positive outlook and renewed energy. Every drop in that bucket makes us stronger and more optimistic.

But an empty bucket poisons our outlook, saps our energy, and undermines our will. That's why every time someone dips from our bucket, it hurts us.

So we face a choice every moment of every day: We can fill one another's buckets, or we can dip from them. It's an important choice — one that profoundly influences our relationships, productivity, health, and happiness.

CHAPTER ONE

Negativity Kills

When we started writing this book, the first question I asked my grandfather was: "Why did you begin studying *what is right* with people?" Don answered my question without a moment's hesitation — his review of one specific case study had altered the entire focus of his career and life. And this study was about as far as possible from a positive or inspiring story:

Following the Korean War, Major (Dr.) William E. Mayer, who would later become the U.S. Army's chief psychiatrist, studied 1,000 American prisoners of war who had been detained in a North Korean camp. He was particularly interested in examining one of the most extreme and perversely effective cases of psychological warfare on record — one that had a devastating impact on its subjects.

American soldiers had been detained in camps that were not considered especially cruel or unusual by conventional standards. The captive soldiers had adequate food, water, and shelter. They weren't subjected to common physical torture tactics of the time such as having bamboo shoots driven under their fingernails. In fact, fewer cases of physical abuse were reported in the North Korean POW camps than in prison camps from any other major military conflict throughout history.

Why, then, did so many American soldiers die in these camps? They weren't hemmed in with barbed wire. Armed guards didn't surround the camps. Yet no soldier ever tried to escape. Furthermore, these men regularly broke rank and turned against each other, sometimes forming close relationships with their North Korean captors.

When the survivors were released to a Red Cross group in Japan, they were given the chance to phone loved ones to let them know they were alive. Very few bothered to make the call.

Upon returning home, the soldiers maintained no friendships or relationships with each other. Mayer described each man as being in a mental "solitary confinement cell . . . without any steel or concrete."

Mayer had discovered a new disease in the POW camps — a disease of extreme hopelessness. It was not uncommon for a soldier to wander into his hut and look despairingly about, deciding there was no use in trying to participate in his own survival. He would go into a corner alone, sit down, and pull a blanket over his head. And he would be dead within two days.

The soldiers actually called it "give up-itis." The doctors labeled it "mirasmus," meaning, in Mayer's words, "a lack of resistance, a passivity." If the soldiers had been hit, spat upon, or slapped, they would have become angry. Their anger would have given them the motivation to survive. But in the absence of motivation, they simply died, even though there was no medical justification for their deaths.

Despite relatively minimal physical torture, "mirasmus" raised the overall death rate in the North Korean POW camps to an incredible 38% — the highest POW death rate in U.S. military history. Even more astounding was that half of these soldiers died simply because they had given up. They had completely surrendered, both mentally and physically.

How could this have happened? The answers were found in the extreme mental tactics that the North

*R*elentless negativity resulted in a 38% POW death rate — the highest in U.S. military history

Korean captors used. They employed what Mayer described as the "ultimate weapon" of war.

The "Ultimate Weapon"

Mayer reported that the North Koreans' objective was to "deny men the emotional support that comes from interpersonal relationships." To do this, the captors used four primary tactics:

- ▲ informing
- ▲ self-criticism
- ▲ breaking loyalty to leadership and country
- ▲ withholding all positive emotional support

To encourage informing, the North Koreans gave prisoners rewards such as cigarettes when they snitched on one another. But neither the offender nor the soldier reporting the violation was punished — the captors encouraged this practice for a different reason. Their intent was to break relationships and turn the men against each other. The captors understood that the soldiers could actually harm each other if they were encouraged to dip from their comrades' buckets every day.

To promote self-criticism, the captors gathered groups of 10 or 12 soldiers and employed what Mayer described as "a corruption of group psychotherapy." In these sessions, each man was required to stand up in front of the group and confess *all the bad things he had done* — as well as *all the good things he could have done but failed to do.*

The most important part of this tactic was that the soldiers were not "confessing" to the North Koreans, but to their own peers. By subtly eroding the caring, trust, respect, and social acceptance among the American soldiers, the North Koreans created an environment in which buckets of goodwill were constantly and ruthlessly drained.

The third major tactic that the captors employed was breaking loyalty to leadership and country. The primary way they did this was by slowly and relentlessly undermining a soldier's allegiance to his superiors.

The consequences were ghastly. In one case, a colonel instructed one of his men not to drink the water from a rice paddy field because he knew the organisms in the water might kill him. The soldier looked at his colonel and remarked, "Buddy, you ain't no colonel anymore; you're just a lousy prisoner like me. You take care of yourself, and I'll take care of me." The soldier died of dysentery a few days later.

In another case, 40 men stood by as three of their extremely ill fellow soldiers were thrown out of their mud hut by a comrade and left to die in the elements. Why did their fellow soldiers do nothing to help them? Because it "wasn't their job." The relationships had been broken; the soldiers simply didn't care about each other anymore.

But the tactic of withholding all positive emotional support while inundating soldiers with negative emotions was perhaps *bucket dipping in its purest and most malicious form.* If a soldier received a supportive letter from home, the captors withheld it. All negative letters, however — such as those telling of a relative passing away, or ones in which a wife wrote that she had given up on her husband's return and was going to remarry — were delivered to soldiers immediately.

The captors would even deliver overdue bills from collection agencies back home — within less than two weeks of the original postmark. The effects were devastating: The soldiers had nothing to live for and lost basic belief in themselves and their loved ones, not to mention God and country. Mayer said that the North Koreans had put the American soldiers "into a kind of emotional and psychological isolation, the likes of which we had never seen."

Studying Positivity

Moved by this story of psychological torture and deprivation — and perhaps inspired by the hope that these soldiers had not suffered or died in vain — Don Clifton and his colleagues decided to study the flip side of this horrific equation. They wondered: If people can be literally destroyed by unrelenting negative reinforcement, can they be uplifted and inspired to a greater degree by similar levels of positivity? In essence, they asked:

Can positivity have an even stronger impact than negativity?

Their research to answer this question inspired the Theory of the Dipper and the Bucket. The theory is based on the following principles.

Everyone has an invisible bucket. We are at our best when our buckets are overflowing — and at our worst when they are empty.

Everyone also has an invisible dipper. In each interaction, we can use our dipper either to fill or to dip from others' buckets.

Whenever we choose to fill others' buckets, we in turn fill our own.

The Theory of the Dipper and the Bucket has been investigated, applied, and embraced by millions around the world over the past half century. People who have heard this theory found it to be inspiring and easily applicable in their everyday lives. Most importantly, it's a theory you can put to work to make your life better — right now.

In the pages that follow, you will find:

- a simple language to use and share with others
- a summary of research discoveries that are applicable in your daily life
- true dipper and bucket stories
- ways to eliminate negativity from your workplace and life
- five proven strategies for increasing positive emotions

CHAPTER TWO

Positivity, Negativity, and Productivity

Most of us will never endure the kind of psychological torture that the American POWs suffered during the Korean War. Yet we all experience positive and negative interactions every day that influence how we feel and behave. Just because these interactions are commonplace and often undramatic doesn't mean they do not matter. They do. While most of our negative experiences will not kill us, they can slowly but surely erode our well-being and productivity. Fortunately, positive experiences or "bucket filling" can be even more powerful.

Bucket Filling in Organizations

Although bucket filling goes far beyond the concepts of "recognition" and "praise," these are two critical components for creating positive emotions in organizations.

In fact, we have surveyed more than 4 million employees worldwide on this topic. Our latest analysis, which
includes more than 10,000 business units and more than
30 industries, has found that individuals who receive
regular recognition and praise:

- increase their individual productivity
- increase engagement among their
  colleagues
- are more likely to stay with their
  organization
- receive higher loyalty and satisfaction scores
  from customers
- have better safety records and fewer
  accidents on the job

To put this into perspective, think about the greatest recognition you have ever received in the workplace.
Chances are, it caused you to feel better about your organization and, in turn, become more productive. Great
recognition and praise can immediately transform a
workplace. And just one person can infuse positive
emotions into an entire group by filling buckets more
frequently. Studies show that organizational leaders
who share positive emotions have workgroups with a
more positive mood, enhanced job satisfaction, greater
engagement, and improved group performance.

One CEO we know, Ken, claims that bucket filling is his "secret weapon" as a leader. He has developed very targeted ways to increase positive emotions in the large organization that he runs. In Ken's frequent travels around the globe, he always stops by his company's local offices. And he doesn't visit to "spy" on his employees or just to meet with upper management. Instead, his primary intent is to energize the people in each workplace.

Before arriving, Ken recalls successes and achievements he has heard over the past few months involving people in that office. As soon as he arrives, Ken casually visits with these individuals and congratulates them. He may offer kudos to an employee who recently got married or had a child or praise someone who gave a great presentation. His favorite line is: "I've been hearing a lot of good talk behind your back."

The most enjoyable part of spreading positivity for Ken is to "watch the energy move through the network" once he sets it in motion. He realized that he could light up an entire workplace with a few brief — but very energizing — conversations.

"I discovered that bucket filling is an extraordinarily powerful leadership strategy," Ken says. As a result of this approach, thousands look to him for motivation and guidance.

The #1 reason people leave their jobs: They don't feel appreciated

Killing Productivity

Of course, there is a flip side. Right now, the majority of us don't give or receive anywhere near the amount of praise that we should. As a result, we're much less productive, and in many cases, completely disengaged in our jobs. According to the U.S. Department of Labor, the number-one reason people leave their jobs is because they "do not feel appreciated."

But the problem doesn't stop there.

One study of healthcare workers found that when employees were working for a boss they disliked, they had significantly higher blood pressure. According to British scientist George Fieldman, this boss-induced hypertension could increase the risk of coronary heart disease by one-sixth and the risk of stroke by one-third.

"There was both a statistically and clinically significant elevation during the time people had the boss they didn't like," says Fieldman, a psychologist and psychotherapist. "People who work with bosses they've really hated constantly for years would probably be quite vulnerable to heart disease because of the elevation of blood pressure in the long-term."

Where productivity is concerned, it would be better for organizations if people who are overly negative stayed home. When they do show up for work, they are counterproductive. We all know these types of people.

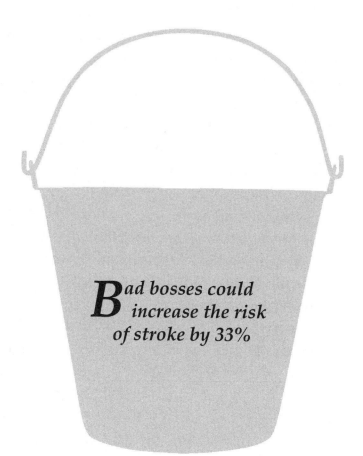

*B*ad bosses could
increase the risk
of stroke by 33%

They walk around the office with glazed looks or move from cubicle to cubicle stirring up trouble with whining, complaining, and even paranoia.

Our estimates suggest that there are more than 22 million workers — in the United States alone — who are extremely negative or "actively disengaged." This rampant negativity is not only disheartening, it's *expensive*: It costs the U.S. economy between $250 and $300 billion every year in lost productivity alone. When you add workplace injury, illness, turnover, absences, and fraud, the cost could surpass $1 trillion per year, or nearly 10% of the U.S. Gross Domestic Product (GDP). These costs are not specific to the United States; they exist to varying degrees in every country, industry, and organization we have studied.

And our figures are conservative. To estimate costs accurately, we only accounted for the direct impact that "actively disengaged" employees have at work. We quantified the productivity — or lack thereof — occurring in each person's own workspace. In analyzing the data, we had to assume that each disengaged employee simply sat in his or her cubicle and didn't wreak havoc elsewhere — an unlikely assumption, of course. Most disengaged employees do plenty of things each day that bring others down with their own sinking ship.

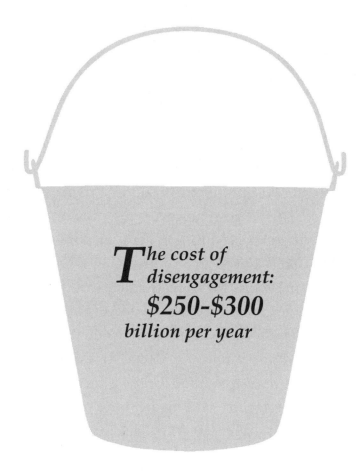

The cost of disengagement: $250-$300 billion per year

Spiraling Downward

To bring these numbers to life, here's an example of the effect that just a small dose of negativity had on one employee. Does Laura's story sound familiar to you?

There I was, standing at the front of the room, ready to get into the best part of my presentation. I had stayed up late the last two nights preparing. I had a great deal of knowledge and passion on this topic and wanted everything to be perfect. And I really hoped to impress my boss and colleagues. Everything was going well as I flipped through the first few slides. Then, a sudden technology glitch gave everyone a chance to start talking for a few minutes.

I overheard Mike whispering to Beth that it looked like I had been out late last night. I wanted to jump across the table and strangle him. Did I really look that bad? I tried to remain composed, but I was shaken.

When my presentation was back up, it was time to get everyone focused again and proceed.

*As I tried desperately to regain everyone's at-
tention, my insecurities grew. Were my first few
points so boring that they were dreading the next
part, or did I look so bad that it was undermining
my credibility?*

*Finally, my boss realized that I was about to have
a breakdown and refocused everyone's attention.
Unfortunately, he did it by saying, "Laura does
not look very happy with us; maybe we should
pay attention now." Ouch! Sometimes I can't believe the things people say out loud. Every ounce
of confidence I had mustered to give this presentation was wiped out. Things went downhill after
that.*

We have all experienced situations when it seems
nothing will go right no matter what you say or do.
Maybe you feel like everyone is out to get you, and you
even start to fixate on negative things about yourself.
Spiraling downward isn't hard to do when your bucket
is being emptied.

Not only do you feel down, but you are less productive because of it, and you bring others down with
you by reactively dipping from their buckets. When
you interact with people on these days, they quickly

sense and are affected by the negativity you radiate. It's not easy to hide — in fact, it's highly contagious.

It is possible for just one or two people to poison an entire workplace. And managers who have tried moving negative people to other departments to alleviate the problem know that "location, location, location" doesn't apply to these people; they bring their negativity along with them wherever they go. *Negative employees can tear through a workplace like a hurricane racing through a coastal town.*

Scaring Off Customers

Not surprisingly, workgroups drained by excessive bucket dipping aren't only less productive and less profitable, they also have higher turnover, more accidents on the job, and lower customer satisfaction, innovation, and quality scores.

And negative employees scare off customers. Think about the last time you called a customer service line and were treated poorly. After this experience, you might have said to yourself, "I am never doing business with that company again." If you were really angry, you might have told others about your experience and recommended that they stop doing business with the company as well. This is the damage one negative employee can inflict on any business.

A *study found that negative employees can scare off every customer they speak with — for good*

Recently, we investigated the impact that a single employee can have on customers by studying 4,583 call center representatives from a major telecommunications company. We discovered three service representatives who scared off *every single customer* they spoke with in a given day — and those customers did not return. It is a serious problem when a company's employees are dipping from customers' buckets. *The company would have been better off paying those three representatives to stay home.*

Fortunately, this study also identified seven service reps who retained and engaged *every single customer* with whom they spoke. Maybe you've been lucky enough to talk with a rep like this — one who listened to your problem, made sure you understood that you were heard, took care of your issues promptly, and left you feeling like he or she really cared about you as a person. Did you want to tell others about this first-class service? And are you still a customer to this day?

The Recognition Gap

Managers, take note: *Praise is rare in most workplaces.* One poll found that an astounding 65% of Americans reported receiving no recognition for good work in the past year. And we have yet to find anyone who reports

65% *of Americans received no recognition in the workplace last year*

suffering from *over-recognition*. No wonder so many employees are disengaged. Although we need and want recognition and praise, the fact is, we don't get enough — and organizations suffer because of it.

Most of the time, organizations begin formal recognition programs because someone in upper management has decided that monthly or quarterly awards ceremonies will help raise employee morale. Sounds good, right? What happens is the old reliable "Employee of the Month" program.

For the first few months, the program might actually work. There are usually at least a couple of people who have been top performers for a long time and deserve more recognition. These stars are appropriately showered with public praise.

But after a while, management struggles with the inevitable question: *Who should be the next Employee of the Month?* Once the executives reach a compromise, a lucky manager must stand in front of the room and say a bunch of nice — and often insincere — things about the recipient. The whole exercise ends up feeling like a sham to both the "winner" and the presenter.

Eventually, everyone — regardless of merit — gets named Employee of the Month. All their smiling photographs appear on a board in the reception area.

But the whole thing is gratuitous, and everyone knows it. The one who feels the worst, of course, is the employee who receives this recognition last. Why wouldn't he? Management waited months, or maybe more than a year, to praise his "great work," which probably feels about as good as being picked last for a team in gym class.

Of course, some organizations do provide meaningful, deserved, and individualized recognition. (In Chapter Six, we provide suggestions on how your organization can do just that.)

Sincere and meaningful bucket filling increases the morale of any organization. Managers and employees who actively spread positive emotions, even in small doses, will see the difference immediately. And creating that difference can be inexpensive — or even free. All it takes is a little initiative.

CHAPTER THREE

Every Moment Matters

Usually, we don't stop to consider the impact of brief interactions. But we experience literally hundreds of potential turning points in a given day, as illustrated by Tammy, a single mother with three children.

My day starts with a typical rush. As I am trying to get ready for work, the kids are clamoring for breakfast. Although my eight-year-old and eleven-year-old are content with cereal, my six-year-old is demanding peanut butter and banana on toast. Eventually, I give in and make one piece as requested, and we sit down for a quick meal. After a single bite, my six-year-old drops her breakfast on the floor. I watch in what feels like slow motion as it lands — chunky peanut butter side down. Her brother blurts out, "You made a mess!" Then her older sister says, "You're supposed to eat it, you dummy!" And I chime in too and tell her something she already knows — that she really should be careful next time.

Consider how it felt to be the six-year-old at that moment. What if Tammy had quickly hit "pause" in her mind and given her daughter some positive encouragement instead of piling on and pointing out her mishap? Tammy's day continues:

I finally get everyone out the door and the kids to school — just in time. Then, as I am driving into the lot at work, I thought I had finally caught a break. For the first time in recent memory, there is an open parking spot in the front row. So, I speed up a little to make sure I beat any other parking lot predators to the spot. Of course, the minute I get close, another driver has the same idea. Even though I know in my head that I was there first, I decide to defer to this woman with a courtesy wave, and I head toward the back of the lot. Then, something strange happens on the way into the building. The driver is waiting there, holding the door for me as I enter the building. She introduces herself and thanks me for being so kind. We end up chatting for a while.

In the span of a few moments, the buckets of both women were filled. Tammy continues:

I get into the office, sit down in my less-than-spectacular cubicle, and check my electronic calendar. I see that my 10 a.m. appointment reads: "Performance Review w/Bill." My stomach just sinks; I

*want to run home and call in sick. I know exactly
what this means. Bill, my boss, must have interviewed my peers the day before and asked them
all about my "opportunities for improvement."
Sure enough, the meeting confirms my suspi-
cions. Bill has prepared a list of eight things that
I need to work on fixing over the next six months.
Not once does he mention any of my recent successes, even though I had worked more than 70
hours last week to complete a major proposal. After what feels like a couple days, I leave his office
in a lousy mood. I think to myself: Why do I even
stay with this company?*

In a short period of time, Bill all but emptied Tammy's bucket. She continues:

---

*Later on, I am walking down the hall, and I run
into Karen, one of the company's top executives.
We had worked together briefly on last week's
big proposal. As I pass Karen, she slows down
and says, "Hi, Tammy. That was great work on
the final section of our proposal last week." I am
just amazed that she even remembered my name.
More than half of the people in my workgroup call
me Tamara, which isn't even the name I prefer.*

If Karen had just said "Hi, Tammy," that might
have been enough. But offering Tammy meaningful
and specific praise made her day. Her bucket was

9 out of 10 people say they are more productive when they're around positive people

filled quickly. And the funny thing is, Karen might have thought she was just making a simple comment in passing; she probably couldn't imagine the positive impact.

Our Negative Culture

Most of us want more positive emotions in our lives. We want to feel like Tammy did in her brief meeting with Karen more often — and like she did after her performance review less often. Ninety-nine out of every 100 people report that they want to be around more positive people; 9 out of 10 report being more productive when they're around positive people.

Unfortunately, wanting a more positive environment isn't enough. Most of us have grown up in a culture in which it's much easier to tell people what they did wrong instead of praising them when they succeed. Although this negativity-based approach might have evolved unintentionally, it nevertheless permeates our society at all levels.

This focus on what is wrong is particularly evident in our school experiences. Instead of celebrating what makes each child unique, most parents push their children to "fit in" so that they don't "stick out." This unwittingly stomps out individuality and encourages conformity, despite these parents' good intentions.

And our schools, which are built around "core curricula" that students have to learn regardless of their interests or natural talents, reinforce this kind of thinking. When a child excels at a subject and receives an A, what happens? Rather than recognizing and developing areas of talent, teachers and parents skip past the A and focus on raising the lower grades on the report card. And very few principals or guidance counselors are known for "calling students into the office" to discuss outstanding grades.

A recent Gallup Poll measured parents' focus on their children's best grades compared to their focus on their worst grades across multiple countries and cultures. The question posed to parents was: "Your child shows you the following grades: English — A; Social Studies — A; Biology — C; Algebra — F. Which grade deserves the most attention from you?" The vast majority of parents in every country focused on the F.

COUNTRY	Focused on A's	Focused on F's
U.K.	22%	52%
Japan	18	43
China	8	56
France	7	87
U.S.	7	77
Canada	6	83

Unfortunately, parents get caught up in the "How can I get my kid into college?" race instead of first considering what's best for the development of their sons or daughters. This isn't to say that parents should ignore the F in Algebra. But why not start with a positive focus on the A's *before* working on strategies for improving the F? If parents at least began these discussions on a more positive note, it could make for a more productive conversation.

At least when students graduate and enter the working world, they have the opportunity to do what *they* want — right? This is their time to pursue their grand passions. Well, that may be true for a select few. Unfortunately, the majority of young people aren't selected for their first job on the basis of how well their natural talents fit their role.

Think back to your first career-oriented job, and see if this scenario sounds familiar: Essentially, you were hired for a job, then you were expected to *change who you were* to fit the role. If you struggled, then you may have had to endure a "competency" program designed to "fix the problem." The weakness-based approach follows us throughout our lives, from school to the workplace.

They Missed It

More than 70 years ago, the fields of education and psychology overlooked an important study — one with implications that could have, and probably should have, altered the ensuing focus of human inquiry. It's possible that we've all been suffering from the oversight ever since.

The study, conducted by Dr. Elizabeth Hurlock in 1925, was designed to explore what would happen when fourth- and sixth-grade students in a math class received different types of feedback on their work. Hurlock wanted to find out if it was more effective to praise, criticize, or ignore students. The outcome was to be determined by how many math problems each student had solved 2, 3, 4, and 5 days later.

Children in the first group were identified by name and praised in front of the classroom for their good work. Children in the second group were also identified by name in front of the group, but they were criticized for their poor work. Those in the third group were completely ignored, although they were present to hear the others being praised and scolded. A fourth (control) group was moved to another room after the first test. Members of this group took the same tests, but they received no comments on their performance.

Students in both the "praised" and "criticized" groups did better after the first day. Then their performance changed dramatically. The students who were criticized showed a major decline in their test scores, and by Days 3 and 4, they were performing on par with students who had been completely ignored.

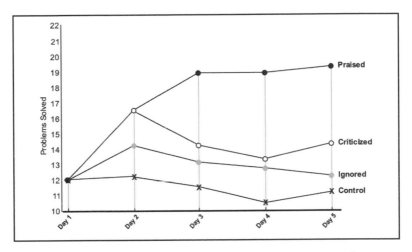

In contrast, the students who were praised experienced a major improvement after Day 2 that was sustained through the end of the study. By the fifth day of this experiment, the group that received praise showed unequivocally stronger performance than the other study groups. The overall improvement by group was:

> Praised — 71%
> Criticized — 19%
> Ignored — 5%

You would think this study caused quite a stir among psychologists and educators. But it didn't. Until recently, the scientific community has focused almost exclusively on studying the effects of negative or traumatic moments. That focus is finally starting to change.

We experience approximately 20,000 individual moments every day

The Emergence of Positive Psychology

As a result of the Positive Psychology movement — the study of *what is right* with people — some of the world's leading academic minds are now devoting their careers to analyzing the effects of positive emotions. At the risk of greatly oversimplifying a decade of in-depth research, many of the world's most noted scientists have put negativity on trial — and have found it guilty.

These recent studies show that negative emotions can be harmful to your health and might even shorten your life span. We already know that one negative person can ruin an entire workplace, but negative emotions can also destroy relationships, families, and entire careers.

In contrast, recent discoveries suggest that *positive emotions are an essential daily requirement for survival.* Not only do they improve your physical and mental health, but they can also provide a buffer against depression and illness.

Thousands of Moments Every Day

According to Nobel Prize-winning scientist Daniel Kahneman, we experience approximately *20,000 individual moments in a waking day.* Each "moment" lasts a few seconds. If you consider any strong memory — positive or negative — you'll notice that the imagery in your mind is actually defined by your recollection of a precise point in time. And rarely does a neutral encounter stay in your mind — the memorable moments are almost always positive or negative. In some cases, a single encounter can change your life forever.

In a recent *Today* segment, Katie Couric interviewed a young man named Brian Bennett who had grown up in a troubled and abusive environment. He had struggled in school and had been picked on regularly at a young age. Now, Brian is a successful and well-adjusted adult. When Couric asked him, "What made the difference?" the young man responded without thinking twice: The defining moment in his life occurred when a grade school teacher simply told him that she cared about him and believed in him. This one small interaction turned Brian Bennett's life around.

In another case, we asked Kristin, a management consultant, "What is the greatest recognition you have ever received?" Her answer: "Three words in an e-mail." We then found out that when Kristin's mother passed away, a mentor at work whom Kristin had admired throughout her career wrote her a special note. Her mentor's e-mail concluded by saying: "Your mother was very proud of you, and *so am I*." After 25 years with her company, three simple words carried more meaning than any other recognition Kristin had received in her entire life.

The Magic Ratio

Of course, few moments are this profound, but even less memorable interactions are important. Positive Psychology experts are finding that the *frequency* of small, positive acts is critical. John Gottman's pioneering research on marriages suggests there is a "magic ratio" of 5 to 1 — in terms of our balance of positive to negative interactions. Gottman found that marriages are significantly more likely to succeed when the couple's interactions are near that 5 to 1 ratio of positive to negative. When the ratio approaches 1 to 1, marriages "cascade to divorce."

In a fascinating study, Gottman teamed up with two mathematicians to test this model. Starting in 1992, they recruited 700 couples who had just received their marriage licenses. For each couple, the researchers videotaped a 15-minute conversation between husband and wife and counted the number of positive and negative interactions. Then, based on the 5 to 1 ratio, they predicted whether each couple would stay together or divorce.

Ten years later, Gottman and his colleagues followed up with each couple to determine the accuracy of their original predictions. The results were stunning. They had predicted divorce with 94% accuracy — based on scoring the couples' interactions for 15 minutes.

The magic ratio:
5 positive interactions
for every
1 negative interaction

This ratio is critical in the workplace as well. A recent study found that workgroups with positive-to-negative interaction ratios greater than 3 to 1 are significantly more productive than teams that do not reach this ratio. Fredrickson and Losada's mathematical modeling of positive-to-negative ratios, however, also suggests the existence of an *upper limit*: Things can worsen if the ratio goes higher than 13 to 1.

So while this book focuses primarily on ways to increase positive emotions, it's important to note that we don't recommend ignoring negativity and weakness; *positivity must be grounded in reality*. A "Pollyanna" approach, in which the negative is completely ignored, can result in a false optimism that is counterproductive — and sometimes downright annoying. There are times when it's absolutely necessary to correct our mistakes and figure out how to manage our weaknesses.

But most of us don't have to worry about breaking the upper limit. The positive-to-negative ratios in most organizations are woefully inadequate and leave substantial room for improvement.

Increasing Longevity

Negative emotions can lead to serious problems. Thousands of studies have revealed the damaging results of stress, anger, and hostility on the mind and body. In

*T*oo much positive emotion?

*More than
13 positive interactions
for every
1 negative interaction
could decrease
productivity*

contrast, positive emotions can buffer us against adverse health effects and depression. They enable faster recovery from pain, trauma, and illness. And positive emotions might lead to an increase in life span.

Researchers who studied 839 Mayo Clinic patients over a 30-year period found a link between optimism in how people explained life events and a lower risk of early death. And a landmark study of 180 elderly Catholic nuns revealed that nuns with more positive emotions lived significantly longer than nuns with fewer positive emotions. The researchers studied handwritten autobiographies each woman had written in her early twenties. The frequency of positive emotions in these early writings was scored and compared to mortality rates for these women when they were 75 to 95 years old.

The results were staggering. The nuns who reported experiencing more positive emotions lived, on average, about 10 years longer. Even more startling was the fact that 25 nuns in the group with fewer positive emotions had passed away at the time of the study, compared with only 10 deaths in the group with more positive emotions.

To put this in perspective, consider that cigarette smoking has been shown to reduce life expectancy by 5.5 years for males and 7 years for females. So, negative emotions might cut more years off of life expectancy

Extending longevity: Increasing positive emotions could lengthen life span by 10 years

than smoking. There's no surgeon general's warning about negative emotions, but there should be.

Physical and Mental Health Effects

In addition to extending our life span, positive emotions can improve our daily physical and mental well-being. A study of Harvard graduates revealed that the way in which young men explained negative events — pessimistically or optimistically — predicted several physical health outcomes decades later. Specifically, *optimism early in life predicted good health later in life.*

Other studies suggest that optimism can ward off and shorten the duration of the common cold. Based on studies that analyzed blood counts, optimists were found to have more T4 or "helper" cells that fight against infection. Optimists have also been found to average less than one doctor visit per year, while pessimists average more than 3.5 visits per year. Increasing the positive emotions in your life might even help to minimize your healthcare costs.

It's clear that positive emotions directly affect our physical health, but what about our mental health and interactions with others?

Barbara Fredrickson, director of the Positive Emotions and Psychophysiology Laboratory at the University of Michigan, has done a great deal of research on this subject. She reports, "Positive emotions do much more than merely signal well-being. Positive emotions also improve coping and produce well-being. They do so not just in the present, pleasant moment, but over the long term as well. . . . *Positive emotions are not trivial luxuries, but instead may be critical necessities for optimal functioning.*"

Indeed, Fredrickson concludes that positive emotions:

- protect us from, and can undo the effects of, negative emotions

- fuel resilience and can transform people

- broaden our thinking, encouraging us to discover new lines of thought or action

- break down racial barriers

- build durable physical, intellectual, social, and psychological resources that can function as "reserves" during trying times

- produce optimal functioning in organizations and individuals

- improve the overall performance of a group (when leaders express more positive emotions)

It appears that science is just now beginning to scratch the surface on this topic. After centuries of studying mental illness, experts are finally investigating and attempting to measure mental wellness.

CHAPTER FOUR

Tom's Story: An Overflowing Bucket

As you read this book, you may be wondering: "Isn't being positive or negative genetic and somewhat hard to change?" The short answer is "Yes." We all know people who seem to be (and probably are) born with a negative predisposition. And you undoubtedly have met people who seem innately, irrepressibly positive.

The scientific community has varying views on this matter. Some studies suggest that positivity and negativity are primarily rooted in nature; others argue for nurture. The most common theory right now is that both nature and nurture make a significant, and possibly equal, contribution.

Noted psychologist Ed Diener describes how our capacity for happiness has a "baseline" measure, much like our physical weight. Just as some people are predisposed to be thin no matter what they eat, some have a natural tendency to be happier than others. But our level of positive emotions can certainly rise or fall a great deal based on what happens to us over time. And it would not hurt most of us to go on a diet consisting of more positive emotions and fewer negative emotions.

Regardless of an individual's innate starting point, regular bucket filling can increase his or her positive emotions. To illustrate the long-term impact, we decided to share a personal story.

A Birthday Present

Shortly after we started working on this book, I realized that Don's birthday was right around the corner. Since we were creating a book about positive emotions, I decided to write him a letter detailing the importance of bucket filling in my own life. I figured this birthday present would have more meaning than a standard gift. And knowing that Don was facing an uphill battle with cancer, I thought this was the right time to express my appreciation and gratitude.

When I was very young, I remember Don saying that we should gather to celebrate all the great things that a person has done — while they are still around to be part of the celebration. When he went to funerals, it bothered him that so many people waited until they were eulogizing a loved one to liberally fill his or her bucket. "Why not do this while they are alive?" he would ask.

So on Don's 79th birthday, I shared my personal story with him. When he read it, he was moved to tears. A few days later, Don asked if I would consider sharing my story in this book. He thought it would be a good illustration of continuous bucket filling, and I agreed.

What follows is the story I gave to Don on his birthday. It is an account of how regular bucket filling shaped my own life while I was growing up.

Searching for Early Traces of Talent

As the first child of my generation in a large, extended family, I benefited from a unique method of child rearing. It certainly defied the conventional wisdom at that time. From the day I was born, each member of my family was determined to help me focus on what I did best. They provided constant support and encouragement.

By the time I turned four, my mother and grandmother had spotted my keen interest in reading. So they would sit with me for hours on end, helping me learn to read. This teaching, nurturing, and attention made a real difference.

Whenever relatives dropped by, they would ask what I was reading or pose specific questions about activities I enjoyed. It is now easy to see they were looking for early cues to my natural yearnings and talents. The minute my family noticed my passion in a certain area, they encouraged me to learn as much as possible on that topic. They were never shy with their praise and always quick to compliment even the smallest accomplishments.

Then, when I was about eight or nine, the bucket fillers who surrounded me noticed my entrepreneurial spirit, and they could tell that I enjoyed leading my peers. So when I was 10, my grandfather (Don) suggested starting my own business. I loved the idea and decided to open a snack stand. As always, the rest of my family was thrilled to help me pursue a new passion, and they rallied around this project.

After a few months, this little enterprise was doing well. "Biz Kids" had enough business to move beyond buying from the local wholesale club, and a major candy distributor agreed to give our company a bulk rate and deliver to our location. We eventually moved beyond snacks, expanding into selling apparel and small merchandise. By the time I was 12, the operation employed more than 20 of my classmates, and we had made a couple thousand dollars in real profit to share among ourselves. After a few years in business, this story landed on the cover of the local newspaper and was picked up by national news wires.

All of the caring, attention, and genuine bucket filling were making a major difference in my life. My bucket was overflowing, and this allowed me to concentrate on filling the buckets of everyone around me. At the end of each month, I would give out awards and commission checks based on how much each person had sold. It was fun to watch as my own bucket filling lifted the spirits of my friends, family members, and very young coworkers.

This focus on positive encouragement continued throughout my education. My parents asked about my favorite classes and extracurricular activities on a daily basis. And instead of dipping from my bucket when I wasn't doing well in music or art courses, they encouraged me to focus more time on the areas that gave me personal satisfaction.

They noticed that I was quite analytical and enjoyed numbers and current events, so they recommended that I spend more time studying mathematics and the social sciences. Even though I was already an A student in those areas, my family realized there would be a greater return on my education if I devoted more time to subjects for which I had a natural passion.

Unlike most of my teachers and my friends' parents, my parents were *not* determined to make me well-rounded. Given that my rhythm seems to have been surgically removed at birth, they understood that pushing me to be a better musician was fruitless; I might get to average at best. A popular saying in my home was this age-old maxim: "Never try to teach a pig to sing. It wastes your time and it annoys the pig." As a young student, I found this quite liberating. I didn't have to try to be good at everything. Instead, I was able to strive for greatness in my areas of natural talent.

A Safe and Welcoming Home

In contrast to my own home, I recall how strange it felt when I visited a friend's house in grade school. We would walk in the door, filled with after-school energy. And the first thing his mother would say was always along the lines of:

"Did I say you could have a friend over?"
"Did you get in trouble at school again?"
"You better not have flunked that test!"

Maybe what she said was warranted sometimes. But I was amazed that the first thing out of his mom's mouth was always so negative. Another one of my classmates would arrive home each day to find a handwritten list of negative notes on her bed with phrases like "You need to improve your attitude." These were not very welcoming environments, especially when I was used to going to my house and hearing things like:

"How was school today?"

"What do you feel like doing this afternoon?"

"Do you want to show me any of the work that you did today?"

"Did you guys get to play basketball (our favorite sport) *in gym class today?"*

At first, I thought these friends must have had troubled families. But over time, I found out this was common. In hindsight, I wonder if this explains why my friends and I spent so much time at my house while growing up. When we were there, our buckets were filled with positive support and encouragement. My house was a kind of "home base" where we could go to refuel on positive emotions before returning to the negativity-laden real world.

Confronting a Major Challenge

My life continued to unfold in this positive way — until I was 16. At that point, I started experiencing poor vision in my left eye and confronted my first big life obstacle.

Doctors discovered multiple tumors in my eye and performed several major surgeries. A year later, all sight in my left eye had been lost — permanently. On top of that, the condition indicated a possible "genetic abnormality" that causes sporadic tumors to grow throughout the body. The results of a DNA test confirmed that I had this extremely rare disorder: von Hippel-Lindau disease. As a result, tumors were likely to show up in my pancreas, kidneys, eardrums, adrenal glands, brain, and spine with no advance warning.

Upon hearing this news for the first time, I was shocked and nervous. But, on some level, I was surprised by how little the news dampened my spirits. From that day forward, instead of dwelling on the negative or uncontrollable aspects of this disease, my family helped me focus on what *could* be done. Although there was a strong degree of apprehension in my mind, I never got depressed. At a crucial moment, that kind of genuine caring and positivity had a remarkable influence.

Within the first week of finding out about my condition, I immersed myself in learning how to manage and live with this disorder. When friends would ask me about losing vision in my left eye, I would be quick to point out that the vision in my right eye was 20/10, much better than average.

Looking back, the key was not viewing my prognosis as any type of curse or death sentence. Instead, I saw it as an opportunity to be proactive and stay on top of my physical health.

After continuing to learn more about this rare disease, I discovered that most of the tumors associated with my condition were manageable with early detection and treatment. I resolved to measure my progress with regular scans and checkups.

In the meantime, things continued almost exactly as they had before — socially, athletically, and scholastically. My everyday life did not change. Over the next several years, the only time I thought about my condition was every 6 to 12 months, when it was time for medical checkups. Sure, waiting for the results of my MRI and CAT scans made me anxious. But I managed to keep those feelings in perspective. In many ways, my confidence and spirit were stronger than ever.

My approach was to confront these challenges head-on. I'm not sure I was totally conscious of my attitude at the time, but I didn't let these problems overwhelm me. A decade later, my close friends would admit how frightened and concerned they were for me during that time. But they also recall being mystified by my positive attitude. Although they knew that I stayed on top of things, they could not believe my lack of day-to-day worries about this condition. In retrospect, it was as if I had acquired some strange type of mental immunity that no one could understand.

But there was nothing strange or incomprehensible about it: The daily drops in my bucket from friends and family had *built a reserve in my bucket that was sustainable during tough times.*

A Surplus of Positive Emotions

While I was in high school, my family members continued to point out specific strengths they would notice, which helped a great deal in shaping my priorities and ambitions. By my junior year of high school, it was clear to me that I wanted to study psychology in college. I loved research and learning about what makes people tick. So I searched out and applied to schools across the nation with strong psychology programs. Of course, my family was incredibly supportive of my going away to college. They helped with applications and went with me on visits to several schools.

My family's positive support enabled me to quickly adjust to a new college environment. Even though they were more than a thousand miles away, they still managed to fill my bucket on a regular basis. During my first three years of college, everything went smoothly.

Unfortunately, there were more challenges ahead.

In my senior year of college, an exam revealed a tumor in one of my adrenal glands. Five years later, doctors found cancerous tumors in my kidney. While working on this book, scans revealed several new tumors on my pancreas, adrenal glands, and spinal cord.

In each case, there was some fear and initial frustration. But my most memorable reaction was a sense of relief in knowing that these tumors were caught before they could metastasize and spread to other organs. My vigilance and awareness of the disease had paid off. Each condition could be managed with surgery. So I reviewed as many articles as I could find on each condition, wanting to fully understand my surgical options and the associated risks. All of my energy was focused on what *could* be done. My energy was not focused on what had already occurred or aspects beyond my control.

To this day, I have never stopped in my tracks and asked, *"Why did all of this happen to me?"* I mean it. I may have been frustrated, but I never railed against fate — and there's a big difference between the two.

Personally, I saw no good reason to sit around and dwell on the negative or feel sorry for myself in these situations. It would get me nowhere. Besides, such wallowing could have worsened my emotional and physical health.

Although the threat of facing various forms of cancer is with me every day, I see no alternative other than to focus on what can be done next to stay ahead of this disease. And I can honestly say that it's easy to maintain this attitude on a daily basis.

Why? That's simple: After almost three decades of life, I cannot recall a single day when my bucket wasn't filled over and over again by family members and friends.

We All Need Full Buckets

My case is obviously an extreme example of bucket filling. It might even sound contrived to me if I were reading this story for the first time. But let me reassure you that every word is true. Given my ongoing physical challenges, this high-dose bucket filling has literally been a lifesaver.

We are all certain to face major challenges as we progress through life. Often, we feel as if we were "dealt a bad hand" and that life is unfair. But we don't have to allow ourselves to be defined by our hardships. Our responses to difficult events and our emotional state are much more important. Positive reinforcement about our strengths can buffer us against getting over-whelmed with the negative. And understanding what we do best allows us not only to survive, but grow, in the face of adversity.

CHAPTER FIVE

Making it Personal

The personal story you just read is admittedly unusual, but there are countless examples of people whose lives were made better and more productive by frequent bucket filling. In fact, you can see this happening in great workplaces all the time.

Remember that customer service representative in Chapter Two who treated you so well when you called in with a problem? Let's say you were so impressed that you asked for his name. And let's also say that you called back later to tell "Ted's" supervisor what he had done to win you over. As you were giving details about his "friendly voice" or "efficient problem-solving technique," his supervisor was scribbling notes as fast as he possibly could.

Thirty minutes later, as Ted completed a call in which he won over yet another irate customer (yes, he does this all day), he got a new e-mail message from his boss.

The first thing Ted noticed when he opened the message was that his boss had copied a group of Ted's closest friends from work on the e-mail. The subject line read: "You Made a Difference Today." Ted's eyes immediately moved to the text of the message, where his supervisor described exactly what Ted had done to win you over. As he detailed the scenario for Ted and his peers, he dropped in several direct quotes from your conversation. Ted's supervisor ended the note by explaining how Ted's actions not only satisfied a customer but also "made that person's day a lot easier."

As Ted was reading the note, he could barely contain the giant grin on his face. Though fatigued from a long workday in which multiple customers berated him, he was suddenly rejuvenated by the message.

Ted's boss knew the key to great bucket filling: *Recognition is most appreciated and effective when it is individualized, specific, and deserved.* Clearly, he understood that writing an e-mail and copying Ted's peers would cause Ted's bucket to overflow. And perhaps Ted's boss also knows that the same approach won't work for Ted's colleagues, some of whom may prefer a quiet pat on the back or perhaps more boisterous praise in a meeting.

The point is, there are unique and specific ways to fill each person's bucket — and most certainly inappropriate ways as well. Generic, one-size-fits-all awards don't work. Neither does recognition that seems forced or false.

And sometimes the recognition you think will inspire an employee backfires in the worst — and most public — way.

The Nightmare Scenario

Consider the true story of Susan, a manager, and her stellar customer service representative, Matt. The following events transpired at a large insurance company that Gallup consulted with in the 1980s. When Susan became a division manager in this organization, she quickly learned that her success would hinge on her ability to inspire her customer service group toward better performance.

At one point in her career, Susan was a customer service rep herself, and she just loved to win big awards and hear the ovations when she stood up in front of a crowd of her colleagues. During the workday, she would look up at some of her favorite plaques on the wall and remember the rush she felt from winning an award. That really got her going.

So, Susan decided to set up a major awards ceremony to recognize her customer service reps. She held the event at the finest hotel in the city. She invited all of the reps and their families to the celebration, and she hired a well-known speaker and some first-class entertainers.

The last portion of the program was the major year-end recognition for the individual reps with the best annual performances. To further highlight Matt, the top producer, Susan would save his award for last. She wanted that presentation to be the night's main event. The drape-covered easel on the stage inspired a lot of chatter and anticipation.

Susan hoped this award would motivate Matt for years to come, so before announcing that Matt was the top producer, Susan detailed a long list of all the star employee's accomplishments and showered him with praise. Then, she pulled the drape off the award and held the prize over her head as she read Matt's name. This was the moment Susan had been scripting in her head for the past few weeks. She had even imagined the delighted look on Matt's face.

To Susan's amazement, just the opposite happened: *Matt was furious!* The painful expression on his face and his hostile body language spoke volumes.

The angry rep walked to the microphone and proceeded to tell the group that he didn't even want the award — it was just a plaque and had no meaning for him. Plus, he had a bunch already; he didn't need one more.

It was the worst night of Susan's life. Not only had this debacle hurt the morale of the group, Susan now needed to figure out a way to win back her best customer service representative. So, after Susan got over the shock of the whole affair, she started to think about how she could acknowledge Matt in the future.

A One-Size-Does-Not-Fit-All Approach

Susan started by learning more about Matt. She discovered that this star employee loved nothing more than his two young daughters. Whenever Matt talked about them, his face lit up. At the office, he was always showing off the newest pictures of his daughters.

The next year, Matt was again one of the top customer service reps. Susan was determined to get the awards ceremony right. She had called Matt's wife and asked her to take the two girls to the best photographer in the area for a formal portrait, and to keep it a secret.

When the big night rolled around, everything was in place. Susan began the ceremony by talking about a very special man. She described not only the top customer service rep, but the passionate family man as well. Then, Susan unveiled the beautiful portrait of Matt's two lovely daughters.

Matt immediately rushed toward the stage and embraced Susan. His eyes were filled with tears. Everyone in the room was moved. Matt couldn't have imagined a more meaningful and personal kind of recognition. It changed the way he looked at his boss and job forever.

Individualize, Individualize, Individualize

The lesson here is clear: If you want people to understand that you value their contributions and that they are important, the recognition and praise you provide must have meaning that is specific to each individual.

Not only is individualized bucket filling more effective in boosting productivity in the workplace, it builds sustainable relationships and changes people's lives forever.

CHAPTER SIX

Five Strategies for Increasing Positive Emotions

To increase positive emotions in your life and others' lives, you must make a habit of filling buckets. This isn't news to you; by now, we know that our relationships, careers, and lives will be much more fulfilling if we increase the flow of positive emotions around us.

But just *knowing* this isn't enough. Like any goal in life, you must have specific, actionable plans to transform good intentions into reality. So we examined our database of more than 4,000 open-ended interview responses on this topic and narrowed the list down to the five strategies that are most likely to produce results.

The Five Strategies

STRATEGY ONE
Prevent Bucket Dipping

STRATEGY TWO
Shine a Light on What Is Right

STRATEGY THREE
Make Best Friends

STRATEGY FOUR
Give Unexpectedly

STRATEGY FIVE
Reverse the Golden Rule

STRATEGY ONE

Prevent Bucket Dipping

Just as we have to start eliminating debt before we can truly save, we must start to eliminate bucket dipping before we can truly begin to fill buckets.

After hearing the Theory of the Dipper and the Bucket, one man we know decided to put it to the test. He was looking for a way to eliminate his own dipping from others' buckets. So he developed a simple habit of asking himself if he was adding to or taking from the other person's bucket in each interaction. He told us it was a difficult habit to get into at first, but after some time, he realized it was working. By catching himself before he uttered a negative comment — and in some cases making a more positive one instead — he started making himself, and the people around him, feel better.

For the next few days, try to catch yourself in the act of bucket dipping — then stop it. Consider your most recent interactions. Have you poked fun at someone? Touched on an insecurity? Blatantly pointed out something that person does wrong? If so, try and push the "pause" button in your head next time.

Once you've successfully curtailed your own bucket dipping, encourage similar changes among those around you. Are people in your workgroup or school chronically criticizing or mocking others? Do you ever notice them teaming up and "group dipping" from someone's bucket? The next time you see bucket dipping in progress, do something about it. Convince others that unwarranted negativity only makes matters worse.

The reality is that some persistently negative or hurtful people simply won't change, despite your best efforts. They've got long-handled dippers, and they intend to use them. If serving as an example won't help, then steer clear of these kinds of people as much as possible — for your own well-being and emotional health.

Once you've consciously started to eliminate bucket dipping, keep track of your progress by *scoring your interactions*. That's right: Reflect on your last few exchanges with another person. Decide if, overall, each interaction was more positive or negative. Score each one as either a "+" or "-" in your head. Write them down if you need to. We've provided a worksheet on our Web site at www.bucketbook.com to help.

Were the majority of those interactions positive or negative?

Now, as you consider what it would take to fill the buckets of your friends, family, coworkers, and others, ask yourself: "What would it take for me to reach that 'magic ratio' of five positive interactions for every one negative interaction that I read about in Chapter Three?"

STRATEGY TWO

Shine a Light on What Is Right

Each interaction gives us the chance to shine a light on what's right — and fill a bucket.

A friend of ours recently discovered the power of focusing on *what is right*. Unhappy in her marriage, she had been after her husband for weeks to make changes. He didn't seem interested in spending much time with her, and when she complained, he got defensive. So she drew even more attention to the things that upset her, hoping he would notice. Instead, she found that things seemed to get worse.

Realizing that telling her husband how much he disappointed her wasn't working, she tried an experiment: She began to draw attention to the things he did well and what she liked about him. She was skeptical, but she had nothing to lose. What do you think happened? After several days, her husband was happier when he came home and more engaged in the relationship. Eventually, his attentiveness and warmth began to fill her bucket — just as her positive outlook toward him had filled his.

But the most unexpected thing was that she felt happier, on her own, by focusing on the positive rather than dwelling on the negative. And this, in turn, caused her to be much more positive in her interactions with other people. After a few weeks, both she and her husband were passing this newfound energy along to friends and coworkers.

Never underestimate the long-term influence of filling others' buckets. Dr. Barbara Fredrickson says that positive emotions create "chains of interpersonal events," the far-reaching results of which you may or may not get to see in person. But they are there and happening.

Every time you fill a bucket, you're setting something in motion.

Consider this: If you fill two buckets a day, and the owners of those two buckets go on to fill two new buckets, more than a thousand buckets will have been filled at the end of 10 days. If each of those same people filled five buckets instead of two, more than *19 million* buckets would be filled in just 10 days!

So continue the chain: When someone fills your bucket, accept it — never just brush it off and diminish what that person is doing. Fill their bucket in return by saying "thank you," letting them know that you appreciate the compliment or recognition. In turn, you are more likely to share your renewed positive energy with others.

Do you want to see how much bucket filling you do compared to others? On our Web site, you'll find a 15-question Positive Impact Test designed with just that purpose in mind. (The questions are listed on the next page.) The test was created to help you determine if you are filling buckets on a regular basis. We encourage you to complete this assessment right away so you have an initial score that indicates whether you have *low impact*, *some impact*, or *high impact* on your environment. You will also be able to see how your score compares to others, based on results from a Gallup Poll.

Don't be concerned if your score is low at first. This assessment was designed to provide you with a measure for continuous improvement. The questions evaluate key areas of your progress. To be even more intentional about your progress in bucket filling, consider printing the list of questions from the Web site, and use them as a guide for improvement.

Send the link to friends if you want to see how your score compares to theirs. It might be interesting to identify the best bucket fillers in your workgroup, circle of friends, or family. Try it out now, and again in a few months. See if your score improved.

Positive Impact Test Questions

1. I have helped someone in the last 24 hours.
2. I am an exceptionally courteous person.
3. I like being around positive people.
4. I have praised someone in the last 24 hours.
5. I have developed a knack for making other people feel good.
6. I am more productive when I am around positive people.
7. In the last 24 hours, I have told someone that I cared about her or him.
8. I make it a point to become acquainted with people wherever I go.
9. When I receive recognition, it makes me want to give recognition to someone else.
10. In the last week, I have listened to someone talk through his or her goals and ambitions.
11. I make unhappy people laugh.
12. I make it a point to call each of my associates by the name she or he likes to be called.
13. I notice what my colleagues do at a level of excellence.
14. I always smile at the people I meet.
15. I feel good about giving praise whenever I see good behavior.

Make Best Friends

In grade school, kids often stick with sports teams, cheerleading, music, or other extracurricular groups, even when the activity isn't a clear fit for their interests. If they're experiencing no push from parents and having little success, then why do they stay involved? Maybe it's the same reason why employees stay with organizations that are less than ideal, or even unhealthy — they probably have a best friend there.

If you think about it, most of us join and stay with groups, teams, and organizations because of our best friends. We say "best friend" because our study of great workplaces found that having "friends," "good friends," or "close friends" on the job was not as important as having "a *best* friend at work." People with best friends at work have better safety records, receive higher customer satisfaction scores, and increase workplace productivity.

Even though the term "best friend" does imply some exclusivity, it doesn't necessarily mean you should limit yourself to one very close friend. We would even go as far as to recommend that you have several relationships of the best-friend caliber among your workplace, home, and social circles.

Great relationships lead to a significant increase in life satisfaction. Noted psychologist Ed Diener found that "The happiest people have high-quality social relationships." On the other hand, Diener and other researchers have found that lonely people suffer psychologically.

Consider some of your best relationships. They were probably formed through an early series of positive interactions. You're not likely to become good friends with someone if the majority of your initial interactions are negative. Remember this during your first interactions with a new acquaintance.

Start by learning the names of people you see regularly — and for each one, make sure you learn the name he or she prefers to be called. Sure, this may seem like a small thing, but it can make a major impression. It's tough to build relationships until you know someone by name. Your acquaintances may soon become friends.

Whether you want to build many relationships or just a few deep ones, your best approach is to fill a person's bucket in your very first interaction. This is a powerful way to initiate new relationships — and to strengthen your existing relationships. In fact, your friendships are unlikely to survive, let alone thrive, without regular bucket filling.

Put this concept to work today. Begin with the most important people in your life. Tell them how important they are to you and why. Don't assume they already know — even if they do, they'd probably love to hear it anyway. Continue to learn more about what builds them up; be a catalyst for an even more trusting, lasting, and positive relationship.

Listen to your friends with unconditional, positive regard. Support them in their endeavors. Encourage them. Be a mentor, or at least be the person they know they can always go to for a kind word.

But don't stop the process with family and friends. At work, become the person known for noticing when others do a great job. Learn something new about each person you work or interact with. Create positive interactions with acquaintances — even strangers.

You might start to notice that more and more people want to be around you.

STRATEGY FOUR

Give Unexpectedly

In Chapter Three, we mentioned a *Today* segment in which a troubled student described how the encouraging words of one teacher turned his entire life around. Well, there were a few other twists to Katie Couric's segment that morning. As soon as the young man, Brian Bennett, finished telling his story, Couric surprised him by bringing his teacher onto the set. Brian's face lit up as she walked out with her husband, who had been one of his favorite high school teachers.

As it turns out, these two mentors just happened to be Barbara and Mac Bledsoe, the parents of NFL All-Star quarterback Drew Bledsoe. After they visited with one another, Couric announced that she had another surprise for Brian: Drew Bledsoe walked out and gave Brian his jersey and football. Brian was overwhelmed with positive emotions as the result of this unexpected gift.

According to a recent poll, the vast majority of people prefer gifts that are unexpected. Expected gifts do fill our buckets, but for some reason, receiving things unexpectedly fills our buckets just a little more. It's about the element of surprise. And the gift doesn't have to be anything big to be successful.

Luxury retailer Saks Fifth Avenue conducted an experiment in which sales associates surprised customers who were known to shop infrequently with a small gift. Although it was a mere token of Saks' appreciation, the customers loved it, and the sales associates did too. This program helped grow the stores' business by transforming casual shoppers into regular customers.

An unexpected gift doesn't have to be tangible either. It can be a gift of trust or responsibility. Sharing something personal or entrusting a friend with a secret can fill his or her bucket.

In your own interactions, look for opportunities to give small gifts to others out of the blue — maybe a funny little trinket, a hug, or an offer to grab a cup of coffee. Even a smile can be an unexpected and cherished gift. Consider unexpected sharing as well. What books, articles, or stories could you send someone that would positively influence his or her day?

In the spirit of unexpected giving, here is a gift from us to you. We want to share with you something that has already helped more than a million people discover their strengths. It's the product of decades of Gallup's study, it has been used in 48 countries, and it is the cornerstone of several of Don's books, including the national bestseller *Now, Discover Your Strengths*.

It's called the Clifton StrengthsFinder. Don created this Web-based assessment to help people uncover their talents. Research shows that people who complete this assessment and learn about their strengths are more confident, more positive, more productive, and have more direction in their lives. And they are also more likely to focus on the strengths of other people — and thus fill their buckets. We hope that taking the Clifton StrengthsFinder assessment and learning about your natural talents will fill your bucket and, at the same time, make you a world-class bucket filler.

Inside the packet at the back of this book, you will find an invitation card with a unique 16-digit ID code that will allow you to take one Clifton StrengthsFinder assessment free of charge. Upon completion, you will receive a customized guide that will get you started on building your Top 5 themes of talent. We hope you take advantage of this opportunity to see inside yourself and share what you discover with others.

STRATEGY FIVE

Reverse the Golden Rule

In the case of bucket filling, "Do unto others as *you would have them do unto you*" doesn't apply. Instead, we suggest a slight variation: "Do unto others as *they would have you do unto them.*" We devoted Chapter Five to illustrating this point, but we want to reiterate: When it comes to robust and meaningful bucket filling, individualization is key. So when you're bucket filling, go ahead and reverse — or at least redefine — the Golden Rule.

As you learned from Matt, the customer service representative who received the portrait of his daughters, the things that make you unique also determine what really fills your bucket — and vice versa. It's unlikely that the exact same things will mean quite as much to anyone else; some of us prefer tangible rewards or gifts, while others are driven by words and acknowledgement. And while certain people want to receive kind words in front of a crowd, others prefer a quieter, one-to-one commendation or compliment from someone they love, admire, or respect.

Another important aspect of individualization is this: What we recognize in others helps them shape their identity and their future accomplishments. This is why bucket filling must be specific to the individual.

Not sure how to start? Just ask some questions. We've included a few for you to consider. Try them out on your friends. If you're a manager, discover the power of asking your people these questions — and then acting on them. A smaller, wallet-sized copy of these questions is included in the packet at the back of this book, and more information is available at our Web site.

The Bucket Filling Interview

1. *By what name do you like to be called?*

2. *What are your "hot buttons" — hobbies or interests you like to talk about a lot?*

3. *What increases your positive emotion or "fills your bucket" the most?*

4. *From **whom** do you most like to receive recognition or praise?*

5. *What type of recognition or praise do you like best? Do you like public, private, written, verbal, or other kinds of recognition?*

6. *What form of recognition motivates you the most? Do you like gift certificates, a title for winning a competition, a meaningful note or e-mail, or something else?*

7. *What is the greatest recognition you have ever received?*

In addition to being individualized, it will mean more to the recipient if your praise is specific. Putting praise into writing or e-mail is a great way to do this. Written recognition is also especially rewarding because it serves as a lasting acknowledgement — something the recipient can reflect on over and over again.

At the back of this book, you'll find five "drops for your bucket" in a removable packet. This is just one way to provide brief, personalized, written recognition. Feel free to use this system, or make up your own — whatever works best for you and each recipient.

Drops have been used in businesses, schools, and places of worship for more than three decades. Millions of people have used them. Some people have kept the drops they received for many years as a reminder of their accomplishments. Here are a few comments we've heard from people who have used drops:

> *"Drops are compliments. They're a way of telling a person, 'You've done an outstanding job,' or 'Thank you for what you've done.'"*

> *"Drops create positive energy where none previously existed."*

"Anybody can send a drop to anybody else, so it isn't top-down or bottom-up. Drops can come from any direction. This is not management patting someone on the head and saying, 'Yes, you've done a good job, and we hope to get more out of you.'"

"A drop can be a 'thank you' or a moment in time when you caught someone doing something great and understood or appreciated what they did. I think a drop is a way to capture an interaction or moment with someone and say, 'I noticed this about you. I care about you, and I want you to know it.'"

"Try it. Do it. Write drops and encourage others to do it, too. I think people will get excited about the concept and not wait to get agreement from everybody about it. Try it in a small area within your organization and see what happens."

Here is an example of what a "drop" looks like. This is the actual text from a drop that I wrote to Don when I was 11 to thank him for the idea of starting the business mentioned in Chapter Four.

A DROP FOR YOUR BUCKET

11/4/82

Thanks for giving me the idea of starting Biz Kids. It has really helped me learn about business. I think it was a great idea and am very glad I pursued it. Biz Kids is now successful because of your excellent ideas!

Love,
Tom

COPYRIGHT 1970

THE GALLUP ORGANIZATION

Now here's our challenge: Set a goal to write at least five drops or other forms of recognition every month. If you need to, pull out the drops at the back of the book and set them somewhere where you'll see them to help you remember to take the time to compose them. If you don't like writing by hand, you can type them or send electronic drops from our Web site. The site will also allow you to set up bucket filling reminders in case you need a few prompts.

Once you're done writing a drop, you can quietly slip the note to the recipient in person, send it, e-mail it, or read it out loud with fanfare. Do whatever fills his or her bucket most. This is the essence of great bucket filling!

EPILOGUE

Imagine what your world will be like one year after you have engaged in daily bucket filling. We suspect the following changes will have occurred:

- Your workplace will be a lot more productive and fun.

- You'll have more friends.

- Your colleagues and customers will be more satisfied and engaged.

- Your marriage will be stronger.

- You'll enjoy closer relationships with your family and friends.

- You'll be healthier, happier, and well on your way to a longer life.

There is plenty of scientific and anecdotal evidence to demonstrate the importance of bucket filling in our lives. Take every opportunity to increase the positive emotions of those around you. It will make a big difference. It may even change the world.

Don't waste another moment. A bucket, somewhere, is waiting for you to fill it.

Explore the official
How Full Is Your Bucket? Web site

www.bucketbook.com

Visit this site to:

- Take the Positive Impact Test to assess your own bucket filling score.

- Download and print the Bucket Filling Interview Guide.

- Create, print, order, and send e-mail drops.

- Set up bucket filling e-mail reminders.

- Share strategies and stories with others.

- Learn more about applying the concepts in *How Full Is Your Bucket?*

- Take the Clifton StrengthsFinder and discover your top 5 talents.

WE WANT TO HEAR YOUR BEST BUCKET-FILLING STORIES!

What were some of your finest moments at work or in your personal life — when your bucket was truly overflowing?

In your interactions with others, what were your most successful bucket-filling strategies?

If you enjoyed this book, we would love to hear your thoughts, comments, ideas, and answers to these questions.

Please e-mail them to tom@gallup.com.

Share *How Full Is Your Bucket?* With Your Friends, Family, and Colleagues

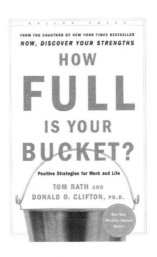

How Full Is Your Bucket? is available at your local bookstore, online retailer, or at www.bucketbook.com.

If you are interested in purchasing *How Full Is Your Bucket?* for large groups or for your organization, please contact Gallup Press about bulk quantity discounts.

Gallup Press also offers development programs, videos, employee giveaways, reselling opportunities, and other promotions based on the concepts in *How Full Is Your Bucket?*

To learn more, please contact us:

Gallup Press
1251 Avenue of the Americas
23rd Floor
New York, NY 10020

phone: 1-800-509-7213
fax: 1-212-899-4899

NOTES

In writing *How Full Is Your Bucket?*, we reviewed decades of comprehensive psychological and workplace research. Many studies referenced within this book have appeared in scholarly works, but rarely have they been compiled in an easy-to-read format. In creating this book, we wanted to distill the most pertinent findings and make them accessible to the widest possible audience. We hoped that doing so would allow thousands more to benefit from the brilliant work of the scientists mentioned in these notes. The page number and a short phrase corresponding to each reference in the text are listed below.

Introduction

12 *During the course of Don's work in the 1990s, a new field of study emerged: Positive Psychology:* Seligman, M.E.P. & Csikszentmihalyi, M. (2000). Positive psychology: an introduction. *American Psychologist, 55,* 514.

12 *Although Don had already written several books:* Clifton, D.O. (1966). The mystery of the dipper and the bucket. [Brochure]. Lincoln, NE: King's Food Host. Food Host USA, Inc.

Chapter One: Negativity Kills

17 *Following the Korean War:* Mayer, W. (Speaker). (1967). Mind control, the ultimate weapon. Audiocassette purchased from Reality Zone and transcribed by Gallup. Available at http://store.yahoo.com/realityzone/mindcontrol.html

24 *Moved by this story:* Clifton, D.O., Hollingsworth, F.L., & Hall, W.E. (1952, May). A projective technique for measuring positive and negative attitudes towards people in a real-life situation. *The Journal of Educational Psychology,* 273-283.

Chapter Two: Positivity, Negativity, and Productivity

28 *Our latest analysis:* Harter, J.K., Schmidt, F.L., & Killham, E.A. (2003). Employee engagement, satisfaction, and business-unit-level outcomes: a meta-analysis. Washington, D.C.: The Gallup Organization.

28 *Studies show that organizational leaders:* George, J.M. (1995). Leader positive mood and group performance: The case of customer service. *Journal of Applied Social Psychology, 25, 9,* 778-794.

31 *According to the U.S. Department of Labor:* Theisen, T. (2003, March 25). Recognizing all staff members is an important task. *Lincoln Journal Star,* p. 4A.

31 *One study of healthcare workers:* Bhattacharya, S. Unfair bosses make blood pressure soar. (2003, June). NewScientist.com. Retrieved August 20, 2003, from http://www.newscientist.com/news/ news.jsp?id=ns99993863

33 *It costs the U.S. economy:* Post 9/11, Compassionate companies had highly engaged employees, reports *GMJ.* (2002, March). *Gallup Management Journal.* Retrieved August 20, 2003, from http://gmj.gallup.com/content/default.asp?ci=478

37 *Not surprisingly:* Harter, J.K., Schmidt, F.L., & Killham, E.A. (2003). Employee engagement, satisfaction, and business-unit-level outcomes: a meta-analysis. Washington, D.C.: The Gallup Organization; and

Cameron, K.S., Bright, D., & Caza, A. (in press). Exploring the relationships between organizational virtuousness and performance. *American Behavioral Scientist.*

Chapter Three: Every Moment Matters

50 *The study, conducted by Dr. Elizabeth Hurlock in 1925:* Hurlock, E.B. (1925). An evaluation of certain incentives used in school work. *Journal of Educational Psychology, 16,* 145-159.

53 *As a result of the Positive Psychology movement:* Seligman, M.E.P. & Csikszentmihalyi, M. (2000). Positive psychology: an introduction. *American Psychologist, 55,* 514.

53 *According to Nobel Prize-winning scientist Daniel Kahneman:* Kahneman, D. (2002). A day in the lives of 1,000 working women in Texas. Presented at the First International Positive Psychology Summit, Washington, D.C. Transcript from voice recording available at http://www.gallup.hu/pps/kahneman_long.htm

54 *In a recent Today segment:* Touchet, T. (Executive Producer). (2003, November 11). *Today* [Television broadcast]. New York: NBC.

55 *John Gottman's pioneering research:* Gottman, John. (1994). *Why marriages succeed or fail . . . and how you can make yours last.* New York: Fireside.

55 *Ten years later:* Cooke, R. (2004, February 17). Researchers say they can predict divorces. *The Boston Globe Online.* Retrieved February 20, 2004, from http://www.boston.com/news/globe/health_science/articles/2004/02/17/researchers_say_they_can_predict_divorces/

57 *A recent study found that workgroups:* Losada, M. (1999). The complex dynamics of high performance teams. *Mathematical and Computer Modeling, 30,* 179-192.

57 *Fredrickson and Losada's mathematical modeling:* Fredrickson, B. (2003, October). Positive emotions and upward spirals in organizations. Presented at The Gallup Organization World Conference, Omaha, NE.

57 *Thousands of studies:* Witvliet, C.V.O., Ludwig, T.E., & Vander Laan, K.L. (2001). Granting forgiveness or harboring grudges: implications for emotion, physiology, and health. *Psychological Science, 12,* 117-123;

Seligman, M.E.P. (2002). *Authentic happiness.* New York: The Free Press; and

Snyder, C.R., Rand, K.L., & Sigmon, D.R. (2001). Hope theory: a member of the positive psychology family. *Handbook of Positive Psychology,* pp. 257-268. New York: Oxford University Press.

59 *Researchers who studied 839 Mayo Clinic patients:* Maruta, T., Colligan, R.C., Malinchoc, M., & Offord, K.P. (2000). Optimists vs. pessimists: survival rate among medical patients over a 30-year period. *Mayo Clinic Proceedings, 75,* 140-143.

59 *And a landmark study of 180 elderly Catholic nuns:* Danner D., Snowdon, D., & Friesen, W. (2001). Positive emotions in early life and longevity: findings from the nun study [Electronic version]. *Journal of Personality and Social Psychology, 80,* 804-813.

59 *To put this in perspective:* Smoking hits women hard. (1999, January 12). BBC News/BBC Online Network. Retrieved August 20, 2003, from http://news.bbc.co.uk/1/hi/health/253627.stm

61 *A study of Harvard graduates:* Peterson, C., Seligman, M.E.P., & Valliant, G.E. (1988). Pessimistic explanatory style is a risk factor for physical illness: a thirty-five year longitudinal study. *Journal of Personality and Social Psychology, 55,* 23-27.

61 *Based on studies that analyzed blood counts:* Peterson, C. & Bossio, L.M. (1991). *Health and optimism.* New York: The Free Press.

61 *Barbara Fredrickson, director of the Positive Emotions and Psychophysiology Laboratory at the University of Michigan:* Fredrickson, B.L. Leading with positive emotions. Retrieved August 20, 2003, from University of Michigan Business School, Faculty and Research Web site: http://bus.umich.edu/ Faculty Research/Research/TryingTimes/PositiveEmotions. htm

Chapter Four: Tom's Story: An Overflowing Bucket

65 *Noted psychologist Ed Diener:* Diener, E. (2003, October). Positive psychology. Presented at The Gallup Organization World Conference, Omaha, NE.

69 *After a few years in business:* Switzer, Gerry. (1985, April 9). Business is elementary for these school children. *Lincoln Journal-Star,* pp. 1, 8.

Chapter Six: Five Strategies for Increasing Positive Emotions

92 *Dr. Barbara Fredrickson says:* Fredrickson, B. (2003, October). Positive emotions and upward spirals in organizations. Presented at The Gallup Organization World Conference, Omaha, NE.

96 *Noted psychologist Ed Diener found that:* Diener, E. (2003, October). Positive psychology. Presented at The Gallup Organization World Conference, Omaha, NE.

100 *Luxury retailer Saks Fifth Avenue:* Suffes, S. (2004, January). How Saks Welcomes New Customers. *Gallup Management Journal.* Retrieved March 4, 2004, from http://gmj.gallup.com/content/default.asp?ci=10093

101 *It's the product of decades of Gallup's study:* Buckingham, M. & Clifton, D.O. (2001). *Now, discover your strengths.* New York: The Free Press.

101 *Research shows that people who complete this assessment:* Rath, T. (2002). *Measuring the impact of Gallup's strengths-based development program for students.* Technical Report. Johns Hopkins University; and

Cameron, K.S., Dutton, J.E., & Quinn, R.E. (2003). *Positive organizational scholarship.* San Francisco: Berrett-Koehler.

SUGGESTED READING

Buckingham, M. & Coffman, C. (1999). *First, break all the rules: What the world's greatest managers do differently.* New York: Simon & Schuster.

Clifton, D.O. & Anderson, E. (2002). *StrengthsQuest: Discover and develop your strengths in academics, career, and beyond.* Washington, D.C.: The Gallup Organization.

Clifton, D.O. & Nelson, P. (1992). *Soar with your strengths.* New York: Delacorte Press.

Coffman, C. & Gonzalez-Molina, G. (2002). *Follow this path: How the world's greatest organizations drive growth by unleashing human potential.* New York: Warner Books.

Curry, L.A., Snyder, C.R., Cook, D.L., Ruby, B.C., & Rehm, M. (1997). Role of hope in academic and sport achievement. *Journal of Personality and Social Psychology, 73,* 1257-1267.

Dodge, G.W. & Clifton, D.O. (1956). Teacher-pupil rapport and student teacher characteristics. *The Journal of Educational Psychology, 47,* 364-371.

Fitzgibbons, R.P. (1986). The cognitive and emotive uses of forgiveness in the treatment of anger. *Psychotherapy, 23,* 629-633.

Fredrickson, B.L. (2001). The role of positive emotions in positive psychology: the broaden-and-build theory of positive emotions. *American Psychologist, 56,* 218-226.

Fredrickson, B.L. & Joiner, T. (2002). Positive emotions trigger upward spirals toward emotional well-being. *Psychological Science, 13,* 172-175.

Fredrickson, B.L., Tugade, M.M., Waugh, C.E., & Larkin, G.R. (2003). What good are positive emotions in crises? A prospective study of resilience and emotions following the terrorist attacks on the United States on September 11th, 2001. *Journal of Personality and Social Psychology, 84,* 365-376.

Hodges, T.D. & Clifton, D.O. (in press). Strengths-based development in practice. *Positive psychology in practice.* New Jersey: John Wiley and Sons, Inc.

Hope, D. (1987). The healing paradox of forgiveness. *Psychotherapy, 24,* 240-244.

Smith, B. & Rutigliano, T. (2003). *Discover your sales strengths: How the world's greatest salespeople develop winning careers.* New York: Warner Books.

Snyder, C.R. (2000). The past and possible futures of hope. *Journal of Social and Clinical Psychology, 19,* 11-28.

Tucker, K.A. & Allman, V. (2004). *Animals, Inc.* New York: Warner Books.

Winseman, A.L., Clifton, D.O., & Liesveld, C. (2003). *Living your strengths: Discover your God-given talents, and inspire your congregation and community.* Washington, D.C.: The Gallup Organization.

ACKNOWLEDGEMENTS

On behalf of Don and myself, I would like to thank the following people for contributing to *How Full Is Your Bucket?* Don passed away before we could work on this part of the book, but I know he would have relished the opportunity to thank everyone involved. *How Full Is Your Bucket?* represents the cumulative knowledge of hundreds, if not thousands, of great minds.

On a very personal note, I would like to start by recognizing a truly amazing developer of people, Shirley Clifton. She is the grandmother I refer to in Chapter Four who read to and cared for me every day as a child. Shirley has always been my favorite teacher and someone I take pride in calling my best friend. To our family, Shirley is the one who has always helped us to learn, grow, and thrive.

Shirley is the rock at the center of an amazing family, and she continues to inspire us today. Don's wife of 58 years, Shirley was his greatest supporter, his best friend, and an amazing lifetime partner. I admire their relationship more than any other I have witnessed. Don spent his life studying what was *right*, and having a marriage that defined *right* made this possible.

Along those lines, I would like to thank my family for their support in writing this book, and more importantly, for the impact they have had on our lives.

Each one of them has spent his or her life ensuring that more and more people will be able to focus on what is right when they wake up each day. This book would not have been possible without the direction and encouragement of Connie Rath, Jim Clifton, Mary Reckmeyer, and Jane Miller.

On the professional side, several individuals are responsible for the creation of this book; *How Full Is Your Bucket?* was not simply written by two people. This book is the product of those we have worked with over the years — at Gallup, in academia, and beyond.

Two people in particular have devoted countless days to making this book a reality. Geoff Brewer was a brilliant editor and polisher of words. And Piotrek Juszkiewicz worked tirelessly every day to ensure that each part of this book was just right. In addition to being the true "co-creators" of *How Full Is Your Bucket?*, they are both exceptional friends and partners.

Larry Emond's leadership was another key in making this book happen. He offered both invaluable insights and big-picture guidance. Tonya Fredstrom, Tom Hatton, Tosca Lee, and Susan Suffes were instrumental in reviewing multiple drafts of the book. Kelly Henry, Paul Petters, and Barb Sanford were amazing proofreaders, editors, and fact checkers. Molly Hardin, Kim Simeon, and Kim Goldberg perfected the layout, and Christopher Purdy provided expert guidance on on design. Bret Bickel led the team of Matt Johnson, Cory Keogh, Swati Jain, and Tiberius OsBurn, who created the rich Web site accompanying this book. Ella Turrentine and Shelley Mika contributed to the Instructional Guide for Educators.

We would also like to thank a few of the world-class psychologists and scientists who have influenced our thinking throughout: Mihaly Csikszentmihalyi, Ed Diener, Barbara Fredrickson, Daniel Kahneman, Christopher Petersen, and Martin Seligman.

As we worked through several drafts, each of the following people made significant contributions: Vandana Allman, Chip Anderson, Debbie Anstine, Raksha Arora, Kelly Aylward, Cheryl Beamer, Irene Burklund, Jason Carr, Deb Christenson, Julie Clement, Curt Coffman, Barry Conchie, Jon Conradt, Christine Courvelle, Kirk Cox, Steve Crabtree, Michael Cudaback, Bette Curd, Larry Curd, Tim Dean, Renay Dey, Dan Draus, Eldin Ehrlich, Sherry Ehrlich, Mindy Faith, Peter Flade, Gabriel Gonzalez-Molina, Sandy Graff, Trisha Hall, Jim Harter, Ty Hartman, Sonny Hill, Brian Hittlet, Tim Hodges, Alison Hunter, Mark John, Todd Johnson, Emily Killham, Jim Krieger, Jerry Krueger, Aaron Lamski, Julie Lamski, Steve Liegl, Curt Liesveld, Rosanne Liesveld, Sharon Lutz, Jan Meints, Jacque Merritt, Jan Miller, Brad Mlady, Andy Monnich, Pam Morrison, Gale Muller, Sue Munn, Jacques Murphy, Grant Mussman, Ron Newman, Eric Nielsen, Terry

Noel, Matt Norquist, Mary Lou Novak, Steve O'Brien, Eric Olesen, David Osborne, Ashley Page, Rod Penner, Mark Pogue, Adam Pressman, Susan Raff, Jillene Reimnitz, John Reimnitz, Jason Rohde, Pam Ruhlman, Gary Russell, Robyn Seals, Cheryl Siegman, Gaylene Skorohod, Joe Streur, Ross Thompson, Rosemary Travis, Sarah Van Allen, Martin Walsh, Jason Weber, Kryste Wiedenfeld, John Wood, Al Woods, and Warren Wright.

Finally, we would like to close by thanking the thousands of associates and friends of The Gallup Organization who have dedicated their lives to studying, teaching, and believing in what is right. On behalf of Don and myself, we offer our most sincere gratitude for joining us in this lifelong mission.

Gallup Press exists to educate and inform the people who govern, manage, teach, and lead the world's six billion citizens. Each book meets The Gallup Organization's requirements of integrity, trust, and independence and is based on Gallup-approved science and research.

HOW FULL IS YOUR BUCKET?

INSTRUCTIONAL
GUIDE
FOR EDUCATORS

Copyright Standards

THE THEORY OF THE DIPPER AND THE BUCKET

- Each of us has an invisible bucket. It is constantly emptied or filled, depending on what others say or do to us. When our bucket is full, we feel great. When it's empty, we feel awful.

- Each of us also has an invisible dipper. When we use that dipper to fill other people's buckets—by saying or doing things to increase their positive emotions—we also fill our own bucket. But when we use that dipper to dip from others' buckets—by saying or doing things that decrease their positive emotions— we diminish ourselves.

- A full bucket gives us a positive outlook and renewed energy. Every drop in that bucket makes us stronger and more optimistic.

- An empty bucket poisons our outlook, saps our energy, and undermines our will. That's why every time someone dips from our bucket, it hurts us.

- So we face a choice every moment of every day: We can fill one another's buckets, or we can dip from them. It's an important choice— one that profoundly influences our relationships, productivity, health, and happiness.

FINDINGS FROM
HOW FULL IS YOUR BUCKET?

- Daniel Kahneman, a Nobel Prize-winning scientist, explains that we experience approximately 20,000 moments every day. That means we have many opportunities to fill others' buckets daily.

- Usually, people remember positive or negative moments, and the neutral moments do not stay in their minds. The optimum ratio to keep positive and negative moments in balance is 5 positive interactions for every 1 negative interaction.

Gallup Research: 9 out of 10 people say they are more productive when they are around positive people.

A Positive Culture in Your School and in Your Classroom

- Leading companies care about positive emotions in the workplace because positive energy can increase employee productivity. Gallup research (explored in *How Full Is Your Bucket?*) demonstrates that by building recognition and positive emotions, organizations increased employee and organizational engagement and boosted bottom-line performance outcomes.

- A study on recognition, which included more than 10,000 business units and more than 30 industries, showed a direct link between regular recognition and praise and specific business outcomes, like increased individual productivity, higher loyalty and satisfaction scores from customers, better safety records, and fewer accidents on the job.

A Positive Culture in
Your School and in Your Classroom

- It is not a big leap to suggest that student performance can be improved by increasing engagement, connection, and positive emotions in the classroom and in the school overall.

Gallup Research: 65% of Americans say they received no recognition in the workplace in the last year.

CLASSROOM
ACTIVITY WORKBOOK

How to Get the Most Out of These Activities

- Discuss the dipper and bucket concepts with your students, and encourage discussion about each activity. Many students will not have thought about what fills their buckets or the impact they have on other people.

- Make the Theory of the Dipper and the Bucket part of your everyday activities, not just something you do on isolated occasions. The more your students adopt the concepts, the more they will begin to use a common language to process classroom conflicts (bucket dipping) and to encourage one another (bucket filling). The power of that common language will become evident.

- Adapt the activities to the age and maturity level of your students and your classroom.

  – The suggested activities can be modified wherever necessary to make them relevant for your particular classroom. Pages marked "Student Handout" are designed to be copied and distributed to your class.

  – Rely on the body of *How Full Is Your Bucket?* for more examples and discussion ideas, especially for high school level students.

....

PLEASE REMEMBER

*you are welcome to make copies
for the students in your classroom,
but not for other classrooms or teachers.*

CONTENTS

....

Five Strategies for Creating a Bucket-Filling Classroom

Strategy One: Prevent Bucket Dipping

Strategy Two: Shine a Light on What Is Right

Strategy Three: Learn About Others

Strategy Four: Give Unexpectedly

Strategy Five: Reverse the Golden Rule

Prevent Bucket Dipping

What is bucket dipping?

Bucket dipping is when you do or say something to or about someone else that is hurtful—or even when you neglect to do something that would have filled someone else's bucket.

How can you prevent bucket dipping in your classroom?

- Teach students what bucket dipping is.
- Call attention to bucket dipping and bucket filling.
- Teach students how to fill buckets.
- Reward bucket filling.

Prevent Bucket Dipping

What is bucket filling?

It is more than recognition. It involves relationships, time spent in meaningful activity, and providing experiences that help each individual know that he or she matters and that his or her life is meaningful.

It is important to note that people can fill their own buckets and should take responsibility for doing the things that make them feel good or "full." We are at our best when our buckets are full.

What fills one person's bucket is often different than what fills another person's bucket. Make sure you ask each person what fills his or her bucket so your bucket filling is individualized.

HOW FULL IS YOUR BUCKET?

What fills your bucket?
Draw pictures or write about
these things below.

HOW FULL IS YOUR BUCKET?
What fills your bucket?

List the things that fill your bucket:
- things other people can do to fill your bucket
- things you can do to fill your own bucket

BUCKET DIPPERS

What do you or others do to dip from other people's buckets?	What happens when you dip from other people's buckets?
What do others do to dip from your bucket?	What happens when someone dips from your bucket?

When I Feel Like Dipping...

When I feel like dipping out of someone else's bucket, I can _____

_____

_____

_____

_____ instead!

When someone has dipped out of my bucket, I can say:

_____

_____

_____

_____

A Time When I Dipped From Someone's Bucket...

Think about a time when you dipped from someone else's bucket. We have all done it. Dipping from someone else's bucket happens most often when our own buckets are not full. Think about what you could have done differently in that situation. How could you have avoided dipping from someone else's bucket, and how could you have filled your own bucket?

_____

_____

_____

_____

_____

_____

_____

_____

Shine a Light on What Is Right

WRITE WEEKLY THANK YOU NOTES.

- Things happen every week that are worth saying thank you for. Teach students to write thank you notes, and have them write one each week. They can write them to each other, to students in other classrooms, to teachers, to parents — to anyone who deserves to be thanked. It is a good habit, and this alone will change the culture of the classroom.

CREATE LISTS OF THOSE WHO DID.

- Instead of making a list of which students did not turn in the homework, make a list of those who did.

- Instead of making a list of which students have not returned their library books, make a list of who those did.

NOTICE WHAT PEOPLE DO WELL.

- In schools, we test, grade, and compare. Some students are good at things that may not be graded, like listening, sharing, or sports. Find ways to point out other important skills and talents that students demonstrate.

Superheroes Are All Around You

- What are the cool things that the people around you know how to do?

__ Karate	__ Sharing
__ Dance	__ Skateboarding
__ Sports	__ Surfing
__ Writing	__ Skating
__ Drawing	__ Hockey
__ Listening	__ Playing a musical instrument
__ Singing	
__ Being fair	__ Knowing about animals
__ Being kind	__ Other
	_____

- What do you appreciate about someone else?

- How can you tell them about the things you admire about them?

- Everyone is good at something. Try to notice what others are good at.

STUDENT HANDOUT

Superheroes Are All Around You

- Create a superhero trading card with the "stats" of the person you admire.

  - Draw or paste his or her picture in the top box.

  - Write the things he or she does well on the front.

  - Write about him or her on the back.

  - Cut out both pieces.

  - Glue the front and back together to create your card.

Superhero Trading Card

Name: _____

What _____ does best.

Superhero Trading Card

More about _____

Detective Do-Right

Your teacher will assign one person for you to watch this week. Someone else will be watching *you* this week. It does not matter who you are watching or who is watching you. Just look for times when the person does the right thing.

1. Watch the person you have been assigned to observe this week. Watch very carefully, and notice times when this person is doing something right:

    - following a classroom rule
    - helping someone else
    - remembering to do something he or she promised to do
    - paying attention when someone else is talking
    - sharing
    - anything else!

2. Fill out the Detective Do-Right Award form with his or her name and a description of what he or she did right. You can also draw a picture of what happened and decorate the award.

3. Your teacher will tell you when you can present the award to the person you have been watching.

STUDENT HANDOUT

DETECTIVE DO-RIGHT AWARD

....

I saw _____ *doing something RIGHT!*

_____

_____

_____

_____

STUDENT HANDOUT

The Weekly Watcher

You will be assigned one person to watch this week. Someone else will be observing *you* this week. It does not matter who you are watching or who is watching you. Just look for times when the person does the right thing.

1. Watch the person you have been assigned to observe this week. Watch very carefully, and notice times when this person is doing something right:

   - listening to someone else
   - helping someone else
   - remembering to do something he or she promised to do
   - solving a friendship conflict
   - sharing
   - anything else!

2. Fill out the Weekly Watcher Certificate with his or her name and a description of what the person did right. Be creative: Use alliteration, humor, poetry, or something else to make your award special.

3. Think about how you will present the award during the award ceremony.

STUDENT HANDOUT

Weekly Watcher Certificate

Signed by: _____

Date: _____

THANK YOU!

You did something I really appreciated.

_____

_____

_____

_____

_____

_____

To: _____ **From:** _____

STUDENT HANDOUT

Cut out the box below. Then fold it to make your own thank you card.

THANK YOU!

Learn About Others

Learning about others helps everyone feel more connected in a school or classroom. You can help your students become more engaged with each other and with the people they spend time with every day.

Here are some simple ways students can learn about others:

- Learn the names of everyone they come into contact with each day:
    - the librarian
    - the custodian
    - the secretary
    - all the kids in their reading group
    - the kids in their PE class
    - new students

- Learn about what fills other people's buckets.

- Ask people about the things that they like.

- Share what they like with others.

- Sit with someone different at lunch.

Learn About Others

Name	Hobbies, special interests	Family, friends, and pets	One thing not everyone knows about this person	One thing he or she is really good at	Best way to fill his or her bucket

Share About Yourself

ME POSTER

On this paper, make a rough draft of a poster about you. Then, finalize it on a bigger piece of paper. It can be a collage, a portrait, a list of colorful words, or an advertisement for a movie about your life — the poster can be anything that helps other people get to know you better. The poster MUST show things that you are very good at.

Give Unexpectedly

- Bucket filling can happen across all levels of seniority and among people of all ages. There are no rules. You have probably witnessed little people filling big people's buckets. Some of the greatest bucket-filling moments happen all over the world when mom or dad gets home from work.

- A great way to give unexpectedly is by giving "drops" or little thank you notes for things you notice or appreciate. As the teacher, you'll have to decide how to make this work in your classroom without leaving anyone out. When teaching about bucket filling, it is an important part of the adult's role to guard against the potential for hurt feelings.

How to Write a Drop

Drops are handwritten, personal messages written on a drop-shaped note card. They're a simple way to share kind words with others, give unexpectedly and fill someone's bucket.

> ### DROPS MUST BE
> ### INDIVIDUAL, SPECIFIC, AND DESERVED

Drops that are not deserved dilute the impact of the drops that are deserved. No one enjoys a hollow compliment. Drops are wonderful because they allow you to recognize even the smallest contributions or improvements.

Teaching students how to write drops depends on the learning level of your students. Very young students may need an adult to write the words for them, but anyone can give a drop as long as it is individual, specific, and deserved. Some students may enjoy decorating the drops or putting them on colored paper.

How to Write a Drop to Fill Someone's Bucket

- Drops must be truthful.

- Drops must be nice.

- Drops must be about one thing you can describe.

- Drops can be thank you notes.

- Drops can be about times when you notice someone doing something good.

- Drops can be about something you really like about another person.

- Drops can be about something you know another person does very well.

STUDENT HANDOUT

A Drop

Think of the person you want to give your drop to. Write something specific, individual, and deserved about him or her on this drop. Then, cut out your drop and deliver it.

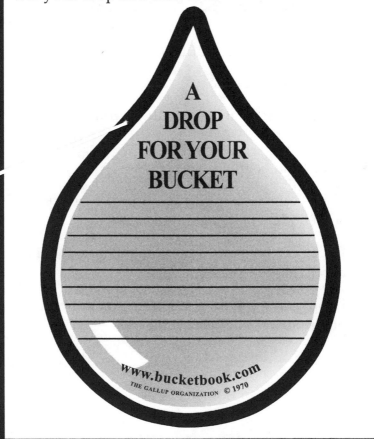

A
DROP
FOR YOUR
BUCKET

www.bucketbook.com
THE GALLUP ORGANIZATION © 1970

Count the Number of Buckets You Filled Today

Check all the boxes that apply to you.

- ☐ I remembered someone's name today.
- ☐ I helped someone today.
- ☐ I said something nice to someone today.
- ☐ I thanked someone today.
- ☐ I stopped myself or someone else from bucket dipping today.
- ☐ I tried to see the good side of a bad situation today.
- ☐ I did something else today to fill a bucket.

....

How many boxes did you check? ☐

STUDENT HANDOUT

Rate Your Bucket Filling

It is not *how many* drops you give, but the quality of the recognition you give. Rate your recognition of others. Give yourself a 1, 2, 3, 4, or 5 on each item; 1 is "not good" and 5 is "very good."

The person deserved the recognition I gave. ☐

The recognition I gave was about a specific thing. ☐

I individualized the recognition. It was something that the person would like. ☐

I found out how the person likes to receive recognition (for example, privately or in front of others). ☐

I thought about the best time to give this person the recognition. ☐

STUDENT HANDOUT

TOTAL ☐

The higher the score, the higher quality the recognition. You should always try to improve your score.

Reverse the Golden Rule

DON'T: Do for others what you would like

DO: Do for others what THEY would like

How you like your bucket filled may be very different from how someone else likes theirs filled. It is important to spend time thinking about yourself, what you like, and what others like. Thinking about the kind of recognition people prefer is probably a new concept for most students and for many adults. It may take a bit of discussion to begin exploring these concepts.

The only way you can be *sure* you are right about what fills other people's buckets is to ask them. You can certainly watch them and carefully try and decode their behavior, but the only 100% foolproof method is to ask and not assume.

HOW DO YOU LIKE YOUR BUCKET FILLED?

Unique Needs

STUDENT HANDOUT

Check all the statements that sound like you.

____ I like it when the teacher tells me about something I have done well in front of the whole class.

____ I like it when the teacher writes me a note about what I have done well.

____ I like it when the teacher tells me privately about what I have done well.

____ I like it when the teacher sends a note home to my parents about something I have done well.

____ I like to be rewarded with prizes, stickers, or candy.

____ I like to be rewarded with awards, certificates, or cards.

____ I like to be rewarded with more class responsibilities.

____ I like to be rewarded in front of the school at assemblies.

____ I like _____
_____

HOW DO OTHERS LIKE THEIR BUCKETS FILLED?
Unique Needs

Think of a friend or a person you know. Check all the statements that sound like him or her. Then ask the person to show you his or her sheet, and see how many you got right.

This person:

___ likes it when the teacher tells the whole class about something he or she did well.

___ likes it when the teacher writes him or her a note about what he or she did well.

___ likes it when the teacher tells him or her privately about what he or she did well.

___ likes it when the teacher sends a note home to his or her parents about something he or she did well.

___ likes to be rewarded with prizes, stickers, or candy.

___ likes to be rewarded with awards, certificates, or cards.

___ likes to be rewarded with more class responsibilities.

___ likes to be rewarded in front of the school at assemblies.

___ likes _____

_____

STUDENT HANDOUT

STAFF DEVELOPMENT WORKBOOK

How to Get the Most Out of These Activities

- Discuss the dipper and bucket concepts with your staff, and encourage discussion about each activity. Many people will not have thought about what fills their buckets or the impact they have on other people.

- Make the Theory of the Dipper and the Bucket part of your everyday activities, not just something you do at quarterly staff development meetings. The more your staff adopts the concepts, the more the power of that common language will become evident.

How to Get the Most Out of These Activities

- Setting a common goal and vision for your school as a "bucket-filling" institution will increase engagement and make your school a more positive place to work. Use the activities in the Staff Development Workbook to demonstrate that goal and vision. The suggested activities can be modified wherever necessary to make them relevant for your particular school. Pages marked "Staff Development Handout" are designed to be copied and distributed to your staff.

- Rely on the body of *How Full Is Your Bucket?* for more examples and discussion ideas. Each teacher (or other staff member) participating in *How Full Is Your Bucket?* staff development activities should read the book before attending.

CONTENTS

. . . .

Five Strategies for Creating a Positive School Culture

Strategy One: Prevent Bucket Dipping

Strategy Two: Shine a Light on What Is Right

Strategy Three: Learn About Others

Strategy Four: Give Unexpectedly

Strategy Five: Reverse the Golden Rule

Prevent Bucket Dipping

What is bucket dipping?

Bucket dipping is when you do or say something to or about someone else that is hurtful—or even when you neglect to do something that would have filled someone else's bucket.

How can you prevent bucket dipping in your school?

- Teach staff and students what bucket dipping is.

- Call attention to bucket dipping and bucket filling.

- Promote ideas about how to fill buckets.

- Reward bucket filling throughout the school.

Prevent Bucket Dipping

What is bucket filling?

It is more than recognition. It involves relationships, time spent in meaningful activity, and providing experiences that help each individual know that he or she matters and that his or her life is meaningful.

It is important to note that people can fill their own buckets and should take responsibility for doing the things that make them feel good or "full." We are at our best when our buckets are full.

What fills one person's bucket is often different than what fills another person's bucket. Make sure you ask each person what fills his or her bucket so your bucket filling is individualized.

WHAT ARE THE CONSEQUENCES OF BUCKET DIPPING AND BUCKET FILLING?

Bucket Dipping	Consequences
Bucket Filling	Consequences

STAFF DEVELOPMENT HANDOUT

FILL YOUR OWN BUCKET

Building up your reserves and monitoring
your own bucket will make you better able
to handle difficult situations. What can you
do to fill your own bucket?

_____

_____

_____

_____

_____

_____

_____

_____

_____

_____

_____

Shine a Light on What Is Right

CREATE LISTS OF THOSE WHO DID.

- Instead of making a list of which teachers still have not turned in their grades, make a list of those who did.

- Instead of making a list of which teachers have not volunteered for some school duty, make a list of those who did.

This takes more time and at first seems less direct. But the truth is, it gives reinforcement to the teachers or staff members who did something right. The teachers who are always on time turning in their grades — or whatever the task is — will be pleased to see themselves recognized. The ones who do not appear on the list will get the message.

Shine a Light on What Is Right

WRITE WEEKLY THANK YOU NOTES.

- Things happen every week that are worth saying thank you for. It is a good habit, and this alone will change the culture of the school. Use the "Thank You!" handout from the Classroom Activity Workbook or make your own. Be creative. For example, wrap your note around a package of candy.

NOTICE WHAT PEOPLE DO WELL.

- Take time to count, rank, and measure success. Have individuals set goals and track their own success. Find ways to reward and recognize successes they achieve. Maintaining a focus on what is going well will fill buckets throughout the school.

Keep Track of Your Success

USING GAIN SCORES

What is a gain score?

- A gain score is any measurable improvement you have made.

- A gain score helps you track improvement over time. It is something you can count, rank, or rate.

- A gain score helps you measure whether the investments you are making are congruent with your professional and/or district goals.

Keep Track of Your Success

USING GAIN SCORES

Gain score examples:

- Fewer students sent to the office each week (a number).

- Fewer playground fights per lunch period (a number).

- Improved school culture measured by fewer teacher complaints or an increase in the number of volunteers for staff development opportunities (a number and/or a qualitative measure).

- An increase in unsolicited parent compliments, for example, about the teachers or school (a number or log).

- An increase in the number of thank you notes you send and/or receive each month (a number).

Keep Track of Your Success

GAIN SCORE WORKSHEET
A Record of Success Goal 1: _____ How I will measure my success: _____ _____ Goal 2: _____ How I will measure my success: _____ _____ How I will let others know of my success: _____ _____ How I will learn about what others are working on and recognize their achievements: _____ _____

Learn About Others

Learning about others helps everyone feel more connected in a school or classroom. You can help your staff get more engaged with each other and with the people they spend time with every day.

Here are some simple ways for staff members to learn more about one another:

- Learn the names of everyone they come into contact with on a regular basis:

    - Gardeners and maintenance crews

    - Cafeteria employees

    - Volunteer yard duty and crossing guards

    - Regular substitutes, classroom aides, student teachers

    - Special education staff such as speech therapists, school psychologists, or occupational therapists

    - Parent volunteers and PTA members

- Learn about what fills other people's buckets.

- Ask people about the things that they like.

- Share what they are interested in with others.

- Sit with someone different at lunch.

Focus on You

Name	Hobbies, special interests	One talent or strength you have (e.g., something people say you are good at)	Best way to fill your bucket

Give Unexpectedly

- Bucket filling can happen across all levels of seniority and among people of all ages. There are no rules. You have probably witnessed little people filling big people's buckets. Some of the greatest bucket-filling moments happen all over the world when mom or dad gets home from work.

- Recognizing when others have been helpful or have done outstanding work can greatly increase the positive culture of a school. When everyone gives recognition, the burden is not solely on administrators, and two important things happen:

  1. Being recognized is no longer dependent on the presence of an administrator.

  2. Recognition is not limited to comments on a job performance evaluation.

More and better recognition happens when more people are given the power to do the recognizing.

Creative Ways to Give Unexpectedly

- Give "drops" or little thank you notes for things you notice or appreciate (a sample drop is provided in this section).

- Give of your time. Spend time with someone who has been asking for your help, attention, or advice.

- Give public praise at times other than "award ceremony" venues (but be sure the person likes public praise).

- Give by following through on commitments.

- Give by listening carefully and remembering the things that other people say are important to them. Then act on something they mentioned.

- Give others credit for contributions they made to work, activities, or programs.

How to Write a Drop

Drops are handwritten, personal messages written on a drop-shaped note card. They're a simple way to share kind words with others, give unexpectedly, and fill someone's bucket.

> **DROPS MUST BE**
> **INDIVIDUAL, SPECIFIC, AND DESERVED**

Drops that are not deserved dilute the impact of the drops that are deserved. No one enjoys a hollow compliment. Drops are wonderful because they allow you to recognize even the smallest contributions or improvements.

Anyone can give a drop as long as it is individual, specific, and deserved. Students, teachers, parents, and classified staff members all can and should be responsible for writing drops.

A Drop

Specific, Individual, and Deserved

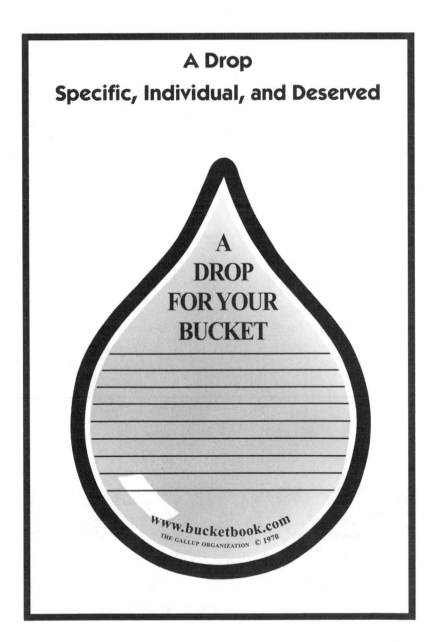

A
DROP
FOR YOUR
BUCKET

_____
_____
_____
_____
_____
_____
_____
_____

www.bucketbook.com
THE GALLUP ORGANIZATION © 1970

Rate Your Bucket Filling

It is not *how many* drops you give, but the quality of the recognition you give. Rate your recognition of others. Give yourself a 1, 2, 3, 4, or 5 on each item; 1 is "not good" and 5 is "very good."

The person deserved the recognition I gave. ☐

The recognition I gave was about a specific thing. ☐

I individualized the recognition. It was something that the person would like. ☐

I found out how the person likes to receive recognition (for example, privately or in front of others). ☐

I thought about the best time to give this person the recognition. ☐

TOTAL ☐

The higher the score, the higher quality the recognition. You should always try to improve your score.

Reverse the Golden Rule

DON'T: Do for others what you would like

DO: Do for others what THEY would like

How you like your bucket filled may be very different from how someone else likes theirs filled. It is important to spend time thinking about yourself, what you like, and what others like. Thinking about the specific kind of recognition you prefer may be a new concept for many adults. It may take a bit of discussion to begin exploring these ideas, and it may take a bit of individual reflection as well.

The only way you can be *sure* you are right about what fills other people's buckets is to ask them. You can certainly watch them and carefully try and decode their behavior, but the only 100% foolproof method is to ask and not assume. Learning about what fills the buckets of the people around you is a powerful way to transform the school's culture.

HOW DO YOU LIKE YOUR BUCKET FILLED?
Unique Needs

Rate each item using a + for preferred
and a – for not preferred. You can use as
many + and/or – as you need.

HOW TO TELL ME
___ Tell me in front of a large group
___ Tell me in a written note
___ Tell me one-on-one
___ Tell me in front of my family, friends, or significant other
___ Other_____

HOW TO SHOW ME
___ Show me with a gift certificate
___ Show me with a new title or greater responsibility
___ Show me with a dinner certificate I can use
    with my family, friends, or significant other
___ Other_____

WHO NEEDS TO KNOW
___ My peers need to know
___ My boss needs to know
___ My superintendent needs to know
___ My family, friends, or significant other need
    to know
___ Other_____

HOW DO OTHERS LIKE THEIR BUCKETS FILLED?
Unique Needs

Now think of someone you know. Rate each item using a + for preferred and a − for not preferred. You can use as many + and/or − as you need.

HOW TO TELL ME
__ Tell me in front of a large group
__ Tell me in a written note
__ Tell me one-on-one
__ Tell me in front of my family, friends, or significant other
__ Other_____

HOW TO SHOW ME
__ Show me with a gift certificate
__ Show me with a new title or greater responsibility
__ Show me with a dinner certificate I can use with my family, friends, or significant other
__ Other_____

WHO NEEDS TO KNOW
__ My peers need to know
__ My boss needs to know
__ My superintendent needs to know
__ My family, friends, or significant other need to know
__ Other_____

STAFF DEVELOPMENT HANDOUT